Small Moments: Writing with Focus, Detail, and Dialogue

Lucy Calkins, Abby Oxenhorn Smith, and Rachel Rothman

Photography by Peter Cunningham

HEINEMANN ◆ PORTSMOUTH, NH

This book is dedicated to Julia for her endless hard work, her patience, and her kindness.

DEDICATED TO TEACHERS™

*first*hand
An imprint of Heinemann
361 Hanover Street
Portsmouth, NH 03801–3912
www.heinemann.com

Offices and agents throughout the world

The authors and publisher wish to thank those who have generously given permission to reprint borrowed material:

Excerpt from *Night of the Veggie Monster* by George McClements. Copyright © 2008 by George McClements. Published by Bloomsbury U.S.A. Children's Books. Reprinted by permission of the publisher.

Cataloging-in-Publication data is on file with the Library of Congress.

ISBN-13: 978-0-325-04724-9
ISBN-10: 0-325-04724-3

Production: Elizabeth Valway, David Stirling, and Abigail Heim
Cover and interior designs: Jenny Jensen Greenleaf
Series includes photographs by Peter Cunningham, Nadine Baldasare, and Elizabeth Dunford
Composition: Publishers' Design and Production Services, Inc.
Manufacturing: Steve Bernier

Printed in the United States of America on acid-free paper
17 16 15 14 13 ML 2 3 4 5

Acknowledgments

THIS UNIT OF STUDY has lived in thousands of classrooms for over a decade. During all of these years, teachers from states across the U.S. and from scores of nations have taught youngsters to cup their hands around the small moments of their lives, to tell the stories of those moments across their fingers, and then to write those stories across the pages of little books. The work that has come from this teaching has been quaint, funny, dear, and, at times, luminous. And so when we set to work on this new series, we knew, from the start, that *Small Moments* would be one of the units of study that would last.

But all those years of experience have changed the unit. It has been pearled with layers of insight and experience. Our organization's (the Teachers College Reading and Writing Project's) thinking about fundamental structures in the writing workshop has been clarified and deepened. And so, when the three of us began the enterprise of rereading, rethinking, and rewriting, we quickly found that although the essential idea behind the original unit would remain, the actual minilessons, preludes, conferences, and small-group sessions would need to be new.

No one has been more helpful than Julia Mooney, to whom this book is dedicated. Julia thinks of curriculum as a story of great teaching and knows that great teaching, ultimately, enables children to be their quirky, idiosyncratic selves. Julia brought her dramatic flair to this book and helped us bring the children and the teaching we were describing to life even as we tried to craft curriculum that would enable children to do the same with the people in their own stories.

We're also thankful to several people who helped us with the project of writing, rewriting, and again rewriting this book. Teva Blair from Heinemann functioned as a counsel and a coach, and we thank her for her ambitiousness. Kim Thompson worked alongside and behind us, helping to make sure that the changes one person made were combed backward and forward in the book, that invitations to kids were followed up on, that bullet points on charts remained consistent across the days. Her detailed, conscientious, and skilled editing (and sometimes composing) made this a far better book. We think of Kim, working into the wee hours of the night to help us, and are grateful.

The teaching that we describe in this book draws on far more classrooms than we could ever recognize, but some teachers played especially vital roles in the latest iteration of this unit. We are grateful to the children and teachers at Grant Avenue Elementary School in the Bronx, NY. In particular, Christyn Sakowich piloted lessons and contributed feedback from her work with her first-graders. We also learned from Sarah Rokhsar, Aida Sanchez-Lobashov, and Lesley Spirka. This collaboration would not have been possible without the vision and support of their principal, Kristin Erat. We thank her for the learning community she has created.

Finally, all that we know about teaching writing has grown out of the extraordinary community of educators that comprises the Teachers College Reading and Writing Project. We're grateful to all our colleagues at the Project, and particularly to some who have played especially vital roles in the thinking that informs this book, including Alison Porcelli, Natalie Louis, Christine Robson, Enid Martinez, Shanna Schwartz, and leaders Laurie Pessah and Amanda Hartman.

The class described in this unit is a composite class, with children and partnerships of children gleaned from classrooms in very different contexts, then put together here. We wrote the units this way to bring you both a wide array of wonderful, quirky, various children and also to illustrate for you the predictable (and unpredictable) situations and responses this unit has created in classrooms across the nation and world.

—Lucy, Rachel, and Abby

Contents

Welcome to the Unit

THIS UNIT HAS, at its core, the deeply beloved *Small Moments* unit from the first Units of Study for Primary Writing series. Although most of this unit is new, the premise behind it remains the same as in the original unit: children are encouraged to write about small moments, and this level of focus enables them to write with detail, including showing a character's small actions, dialogue, and internal thinking. Children produce lots and lots of Small Moment stories and move with independence through the writing process, choosing an idea, planning their writing by sketching stories across the pages of a booklet, storytelling repeatedly until the story feels just write, and revising to bring more detail and life to their stories. A mini–author study helps them elaborate in ways that bring characters to life. You can approach this unit knowing that variations of it have been taught by hundreds of thousands of teachers and have been universally well received. The results of your teaching will be dramatic and important.

The most important advice we can give you about this unit is this: don't wait to teach it. It may be tempting to think that children need first to be socialized into the norms of school, reminded of letters and sounds, acquainted with the word wall, and immersed in wonderful literature, but children come to school eager to make their mark on the world, writing and drawing as best they can. Think about it. Put a child beside a chalkboard or some reams of old computer paper, and what does that child do? She writes. Her writing may be squiggles; it may be just her name, written in four different fonts. Still, the youngster will want to leave her John Hancock, to say to the world, "I was here."

Stories are so crucial to a child's language development that Gordon Wells, after doing a longitudinal study of children's language development throughout their school-aged years, concluded that of all the activities that were found to be characteristic of literate homes, the sharing of stories gave the most essential advantage. "Constructing stories in the mind—or storying, as it has been called—is one of the most fundamental means of making meaning," he writes. Language researcher Shirley Brice Heath, winner of the prestigious MacArthur Award, also suggests that sharing stories is the most important precondition to rich literacy. She advises teachers and parents to talk to children not just about the here and now ("Here is a book." "Stand there." "Move over."), but to use language to help children re-create other times and places. Heath concludes that this "symbolic use of language," as she calls storying, is the essence of school literacy.

Of course, narrative writing is also crucial in the Common Core State Standards. The standards suggest that fully half of the writing that children do across the whole day should be narrative—a very large percentage when one takes into account that all the writing that happens in math, social studies, and science tends to be non-narrative. In this unit, writers work especially toward meeting CCSS W.1.3, writing narratives in which they recount two or more appropriately sequenced events, include some details regarding what happened, use temporal words to signal event order, and provide some sense of closure. There is a second narrative unit in this series—*From Scenes to Series: Writing Fiction*—and by the end of that unit, we fully expect most students to have met even the second-grade narrative standards (above standard for first grade). The work that students do in partnerships in which they respond to questions and suggestions from peers to add details to their writing also matches the CCSS (CCSS W.1.5).

This unit also supports the Common Core's high expectations for the texts that students can read, and writing accelerates that reading development. When a child understands how a particular kind of text is made, this grasp of schema helps the youngster construct an understanding as he or she reads that kind of text. That is, writing narratives gives children an insider's understanding of inference, synthesis, prediction, and interpretation.

This unit is written in ways that reflect priorities that will undergird the entire year. Stamina is certainly among those priorities. One secret to stamina lies in the paper that you give children. We encourage you to start the year by providing booklets—not single pages—each containing three to five pages depending on what children left kindergarten using. For most students, each page can contain a box for the picture and plenty of lines—perhaps four—for the writing. Remember, they have been writing in booklets since kindergarten, so they will expect this! It is impossible to overemphasize the power that the paper itself has for conveying expectations. Within this one unit, you should expect that first-graders will write approximately three or four booklets a week, each with three or four sentences on a page. Those are very rough estimates, and certainly many children can do a great deal more than this, so expect your first-graders to write pages—not a page—a day, and to write sentences—not just a sentence—on each page. For others, the lines are there to push the emergent writer to elaborate and write more than one line per page.

Another goal of the unit is to help children be brave and resourceful word solvers. At the beginning of first grade, your expectation will be that many children write using initial and final consonant sounds, including some of the internal parts of words, and word endings. The writing workshop offers you a forum for teaching students to meet grade level expectations in the Foundational Skills, Language, and also Speaking and Listening Standards. Instruction in spelling is woven throughout the book, and it supports an important CCSS emphasis on phonological awareness and phonics standards including an emphasis on segmenting words into their individual phonemes (FS.1.2d). The strategies for spelling unfamiliar words will help children meet Language Standard L.1.2e, which asks that students spell unfamiliar words phonetically, drawing on phonemic awareness and spelling conventions. At the same time, students will be taught to use tools such as the word wall that began in kindergarten to work toward CCSS L.1.2d, spelling frequently occurring irregular words correctly. You'll guide them to further develop and represent the sounds inside words, stretching out unknown words to isolate and then represent as many sounds as they can with the appropriate letters. As they begin to study spelling patterns, teach them to use this knowledge and their bank of known words to efficiently spell new ones. Support their use of known words and the word wall as they write.

A third goal in this unit is for youngsters to learn to generate and record cohesive, sequenced narratives. If you teach writers to stretch out a story, drawing the start on one page, then the next part on the next page, and whatever happened next on each following page, these drawings will help children stretch out and elaborate their written texts. As the unit progresses and your writers' stories become more cohesive and focused, students will be ready to learn to write with greater detail.

OVERVIEW OF THE UNIT

The first portion of this unit—the first bend in the road of the unit—is titled "Writing Small Moment Stories with Independence," and the title sums up the work that you and your children will do at the start of the unit. The unit opens with you suggesting that children can write just like the author of a simple published narrative such as *Night of the Veggie Monster* (although you could elect a different book in this one's stead, and *Joshua's Night Whispers* is a good candidate) and then giving them three-page booklets and inviting them to story-tell the Small Moment stories of their lives in ways that set them up to write those stories. The most important words of your first minilesson are the final ones: "Off you go. You can get started drawing and writing your own Small Moment book." Convey that you have not the slightest doubt but that every child in your class can think of a story to write, draw that story across pages of a book, and then write the story, too. Be confident enough that if you reach a child's side and he has drawn pictures but not written words, you'll say cheerily, "Great. So tell me what is happening on this page." When the child tells you, be prepared to say, "Add that right here. Put that here, on the paper, so other people will know!"

Teachers sometimes wonder, "Can I ask my students to do this without setting them up more carefully? Without showing examples and providing warm-up activities and leading up to this for a few weeks?" Our answer is "Yes." Decades of experience have shown us that usually, when children are given that invitation to write, they dive in, producing work that shows in a glance what they can do and what they need. Of course, the series will provide you with help for the students who sit frozen, unable to put a mark on the page, but they will be fewer and farther between than you think. Granted, if children did not have a kindergarten writing workshop, some may write in squiggles and dots or may simply record the alphabet or produce strings of letters. But you'll find that others will write word labels or even write paragraphs of fluent sentences. In any case, your response to whatever children do will be, "Read me what you've written," followed by, "Tell me more," and after some appreciative listening, "You should definitely add that!"

This first bend in the unit swings, like a pendulum, between sessions that help children write the stories of their lives to sessions that establish the routines and structures of the class so that this writing work can be done independently. Children will learn to touch and tell their stories, then sketch and write, so that they can move independently through the writing process again and again. They'll learn that when they come to hard words, instead of being paralyzed or derailed, they can use their word-solving skills to have a go at that word. In the same spirit, they learn that when they are finished writing one story, instead of waiting for the teacher to tell them what to do, they can help themselves—or rely on partners for help. This first bend, then, encourages fearless approximation in ways that support ambitious storytelling and a volume of writing.

The second portion of the unit is aptly titled "Bringing Small Moment Stories to Life." Think of your children's stories as paintings. At first, the canvas is filled with a hard-attempted sketch. As the painter gains more experience and is given more coaching and more demonstration, the painter is eventually able to fill that canvas with colors and detail, bringing the scene to life. In this portion of the unit, you will give your young writers the strategies they need to bring the many stories that they write to life. Children will think about whether their characters are like stick figures—standing inertly like little gingerbread men cut-outs—and work to bring the people in their stories to life by making them move and talk. Children will learn to slow down their story narratives to develop each part bit by bit. Since the unit involves a lot of retelling and storytelling, drama plays an important part in this portion of the unit. Partners will act out what the people in their stories did, and then try to capture that on the canvas of their booklets.

The next portion of the unit, "Studying Other Writers' Craft" is a shorter bend, but no less important. Writers continue to learn ways to elaborate on their stories—working to do this both in the new stories that they continue to write at a rapid clip, but also by revisiting their folder full of previously written stories. This time, writers will generate a list of "craft moves" the author of a mentor text made that children could try as well. In this way, youngsters can learn lessons such as the value of writing with precise and powerful actions words. They can learn to use text features (including enlarged font) to shape the way readers read their texts.

The last bend in the unit begins with each child selecting a piece he or she wants to publish. You'll teach a few final revision and editing strategies, and children will put these to use as they work to make their best writing better.

The children will learn to use a checklist to help them edit their selected stories. They'll also "fancy up" their writing by making a cover page, adding details and color to illustrations, and writing a blurb. They'll work with partners to rehearse for the actual reading aloud of the pieces, practicing reading with expression, fluency, and phrasing. The unit culminates with the children reading their books in small groups and then adding them to a newly added basket in the classroom library.

ASSESSMENT

We recommend that you start each school year, K–5, by asking children to write an on-demand piece of writing in each of the three types of writing that the CCSS spotlights. That is, we recommend each teacher devote one writing workshop at the start of the year to asking all her children to produce a narrative piece of writing, another workshop to producing an example of information writing, and a third workshop to producing the children's best opinion writing. If you decide across your school to assess only the type of writing that students will be studying, you can elect to assess information and opinion writing later in the year. But we recommend otherwise.

We're aware that what we are suggesting is not perfect. You'll say to your incoming first-graders, "Welcome to first grade. Let me test you." But here is the thing. Thousands and thousands of teachers have done as we are suggesting and found this to be extraordinarily powerful. So don't dismiss the idea altogether.

Why has this been powerful? First, when you conduct this assessment, you'll come to realize that it's simply not the case that at the start of the year, first-graders are all at the starting gate. From the start, there will be vast differences in your children's understandings of written language, and those differences will be immediately apparent. Then, too, capturing what youngsters know and can do at the very start of the year provides you with a dramatic and accessible way to be able to eventually demonstrate your students' progress toward meeting and exceeding CCSS standards (and the power of your teaching). If you collect baseline data, then when parent's night comes, you'll be able to say, "This is what your child came to school doing as a writer, and this is his latest work." Of course, this means not only that you'll have bragging rights over your children's progress. It also means you will have a way to measure the effectiveness of your teaching.

The details of the on-demand assessment are laid out in *Writing Pathways: Performance Assessments and Learning Progressions, K–5*. We recommend you begin by saying the following: "I'm really eager to understand what you can do as writers of narratives, of stories, so today, will you please write the best personal narrative, the best Small Moment story that you can write? Make this be the story of one time in your life. You might focus on just a scene or two. You'll have only forty-five minutes to write this true story, so you'll need to plan, draft, revise, and edit in one sitting. Write in a way that allows you to show off all you know about narrative writing."

Give children four-page booklets. Because the work that your children produce will end up being looked at as part of a K–5 continuum, we hope that you are willing to give children some pointers that may or may not mean a lot to most of them. In an assessment, it is important that the conditions are kept the same, when possible, so that results can be compared, so although the pointers are not apt to mean anything to six-year-olds, we want to give these prompts now so that everyone is being given the same opportunities. The pointers include:

- Make a beginning for your story

- Show what happened, in order

- Use details to help readers picture your story

- Make an ending for your story

As the children are drawing and writing their on-demand assessments, you will want to move quickly among them, asking any child whose writing seems indecipherable to tell you what he or she is writing and then recording verbatim what that child says so that you are essentially taking down a dictation. Usually teachers record the youngster's intended message on a Post-it® that they later stick onto the back of the writing. Later, when you collect students' writing and try to understand whether their spelling was somewhat phonetic, for example, you'll find that the records of what the writers intended to say will help you decipher what they wrote and what the logic was that informed their writing.

As children get to work, we recommend that you sit among them to observe and note what happens during the workshop. Check to see who is sketching across pages, getting more pages, or rereading. Whose hand flies down the page or makes additional lines to hold the whole story? If some children are writing in ways that you don't think you will be able to decipher, ask those children to read what they have written and then jot the text on a Post-it that you will later add to their writing.

You will see that some of your writers are fledgling writers, while others are writing long, book-length narratives. Expect that if your students were in a writing workshop the previous year, some will, even at the start of the year, already write narratives in which they recount two or more appropriately sequenced events (W 1.3). By the end of the year, your first-graders should all meet, and many will exceed, the CCSS expectations for first grade. Achieving this level of proficiency will require lots of time and opportunities to practice. This unit sets them up to work toward these goals and provides many opportunities for repeated practice, as do the additional narrative units that follow.

This initial writing your students do will provide a window into their knowledge of words and how they work, including letter sounds, spelling patterns, and some insight into phonemic awareness. To gather more information about your children's knowledge, you will probably also want to administer a spelling inventory or letter ID assessment.

GETTING READY

In preparation for your writing workshop, you will want to read *A Guide to the Common Core Writing Workshop* because it brims with suggestions for ways you can organize your classroom, your materials, and your classroom structures. Because this is the first unit in the year, preparing for the unit really means preparing for the writing workshop itself. For example, you will absolutely want to organize a meeting space (ideally a corner carpet) in your classroom and a place to write publicly (usually an easel at the helm of that space). You will also need to organize a way for youngsters to have free access to paper during writing time. Most teachers set up a writing center, with different bins holding different paper options. The most commonly used paper is included on the CD-ROM—and, yes, it matters. Provisioning students with paper that conveys appropriate but robust expectations is important.

Writing Small Moment Stories with Independence

Lives Are Full of Stories to Tell

IN THIS SESSION, you'll teach children that writers use events from their lives—things they do or things that have happened to them—to write Small Moment stories.

GETTING READY

- Mentor text about a small, true moment. We use *Night of the Veggie Monster.* You'll have read this book aloud prior to this minilesson, perhaps on another day, rallying children to love it.
- Sample texts that represent the type of writing students will be doing this year.
  - A nonfiction book that teaches
  - A fiction book, such as *Chrysanthemum*
  - A realistic fiction book
  - A restaurant review
  - Other genres students will write this year (how-to books, poems, songs)
- "How to Write a Story" chart, prewritten with first three steps: Think of an idea, Plan, Write
- A basket brim full of markers near the meeting area. You'll use these to create an incident that can be the source of a class story (see Teaching).
- Exemplar first-grade writing piece that represents the work you expect your students to do (see Link)
- Several versions of three-page stapled booklets, each in a different tray, on a table or bookshelf that will act as your writing center. Booklets might contain two, three, or four lines per page to offer students paper choices.
- Writing tools or a writing toolbox (e.g., caddy) that holds pencils, pens, and a date stamp
- Note-taking system for your conferences—for example, a grid on a single sheet of paper with one space for each child or a notebook with a page for each child, in alphabetical order

COMMON CORE STATE STANDARDS: W.1.3, W1.8; RL.1.1; SL.1.1, SL.1.4, SL.1.5; L.1.1, L.1.2

THE MOST IMPORTANT ADVICE I CAN GIVE about starting your writing workshop is this: don't wait. It will be tempting to think that children need first to be socialized into the norms of school, reminded of letters and sounds, acquainted with the word wall, and immersed in wonderful literature, but that simply is not so. Whether or not your children learned to write in kindergarten, they'll be eager to make their mark on the world, writing and drawing as best they can. Think about it. Put a child beside a misty mirror, a wet beach, a chalkboard, some reams of old computer paper, and what does that child do? She writes. She'll write with marker pens if she has them, with fingers, or with a heel dragged in the sand, if necessary—anything to leave her John Hancock, anything to say to the world, "I was here."

In this session, you show children a book or two and suggest they can write just like the authors of those books. I suggest showing children a book by George McClements, *Night of the Veggie Monster* (2008), but you could select any Small Moment story. Some teachers prefer, for example, *A Chair for My Mother* (Williams 1982), *Peter's Chair* (Keats 1998), or *Joshua's Night Whispers* (Johnson 1994). Either way, the important thing is the message: you, too, can write like this!

Sometimes, teachers look askance at us when we ask them to launch the year by giving children three-page booklets and telling them to write Small Moment stories all on their own. Teachers sometimes wonder, "Can I ask my students to do that without teaching anything? Without setting them up? Without showing examples? Without any warm-up activities? Without more support?" My answer is this: yes, simply ask children to write as best they can. Decades of experience doing this has shown that usually, when children are given that invitation to write, they dive in, producing work that shows in a glance what they can do and what they need.

I have found that children do not need much help generating ideas for true stories. In a classroom that conveys an appreciation for children's lives, children will be confident that others want to hear about the little moments they experience. With just a tiny bit of help, they can easily come up with lots of ideas for true stories. In this session, you teach children two strategies for coming up with true stories, as well as give them an image for the sort of writing you hope they do.

"In a classroom that conveys an appreciation for children's lives, children will be confident that others want to hear about the little moments they experience."

The most important words of this minilesson are the final ones, "Off you go. You can get started drawing and writing your own Small Moment book." Say this in a way that conveys that you have not the slightest doubt that every child in your class can think of a story to write, draw that story across pages of a book, and then write the story, too. Be confident enough that if you reach a child who has drawn pictures but not written words, you say cheerily, "Great. So tell me what is happening on this page," and then, when the child tells you, you say, "Add that right here. Put that here, on the paper, so other people will know!"

Some youngsters will write in squiggles and dots or simply record the alphabet or produce strings of letters with no spaces between them. Others will write paragraphs of fluent sentences. In any case, your response to their work will be, "Read me what you've written," followed by, "Tell me more," and after some appreciative listening, "You should definitely add that!"

Lives Are Full of Stories to Tell

CONNECTION

Introduce the writing workshop by telling children that every day they'll gather for a minilesson and write books like those on the surrounding shelves. Reread a story aloud, like they might write.

Once children were all sitting in the meeting area, pulled close around me, I began. "Writers, today is the first day of this year's writing workshop. Every day at the start of writing workshop, we will gather right here for a minilesson. We will sit in this meeting area because here, we are wrapped in books." I gestured at the bookshelves. "And this year, we'll be *writing* lots and lots of books ourselves! We'll write all kinds of books—true stories like this," I held up *Night of the Veggie Monster*, "and made-up fiction stories like this," I held up a beloved fiction book, "and nonfiction teaching books like this." I held up a nonfiction text. "And we won't just write *books*. We'll also write *restaurant* reviews," I held up a restaurant review, "and poems," I pointed to one, "and songs and *lots* of other stuff! How many of you were an author last year, when you were in kindergarten? Thumbs up if you were. Wow! That many of you?

"Maybe, even though this is just the *first* day of our writing workshop, you guys might be ready to write books—straight away! Writing books takes a *lot* of writing muscles. You up for it?" The children seemed more than game.

"For our first unit of study, then, how about we plan to write lots and lots of true stories—special ones, like books written by famous authors? Listen to one and think about whether *you* could write true stories about small moments in *your* life, like George McClements has done," I said, and reread *Night of the Veggie Monster* aloud.

"It's a great story, isn't it? Did you notice the details? That's what writers do when they write Small Moment stories. They take just a small thing that happened, and they write what happened first, next, and next, telling it with details. I'm going to read a part of the story again, and this time listen for the details that help you picture what happened." I read it again. "Tell someone near you a detail you liked from George's story."

The children talked. Over the hubbub, I said, "Writers, eyes up here." Once I had their total attention, I continued, "You guys are going to write tons of books like this one, about small moments in *your* lives."

◆ COACHING

Here we are on the first day of writing workshop, perhaps the first day of first grade! How exciting! Keep in mind that today's work sets the tone for writing for the whole year—give it all the joy and enthusiasm and adventure you can muster. Try to make it so that if children are lucky enough to have someone ask them about their day, you can bet they'll say, "We're writing lots of books!"

If your announcements create an excited chatter, let it happen! Let the enthusiasm grow with a little, nondisruptive, social energy.

❖ **Name the teaching point.**

"Today I want to teach you that when authors write a Small Moment story, they think of an idea (maybe about things they do or things that happen to them), then they plan, and then they write the story across pages of a book." I brought out a chart I had written up ahead of time and revealed it. (See Figure 1–1.)

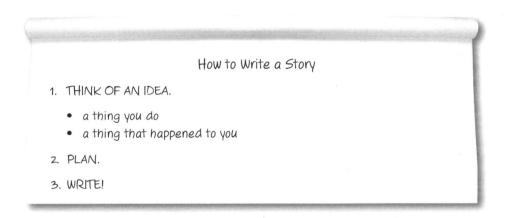

How to Write a Story

1. THINK OF AN IDEA.

   • a thing you do
   • a thing that happened to you

2. PLAN.

3. WRITE!

This process chart is one that you can use across units of study. By leaving space between each step you can add strategies as they are taught. It can be helpful to use pieces of paper or sticky notes for the strategies so that they can be added easily in front of the students and then removed when a new unit begins. The important thing is the students use this as a guide for moving through the writing process, a tool they can refer to any time they go to write this year.

TEACHING

Create a small incident that can become the source of what will be a whole-class, shared story.

"How many of you learned during kindergarten how to go about writing a Small Moment story?" I gestured for those children to give a thumbs up. "Great, then you'll be pros at this; soon you'll all have a chance to think of your very own story and write it." Getting up and picking my way across the meeting area, I walked over to where I had deliberately left a basket, brim full of lots and lots of markers. "I just need to get a marker so I can write my story," I said, and then, as I made my way back to the front of the meeting area with the basket in hand, I spilled the entire contents of the basket so markers came raining down on children's heads, onto their laps. "Oh, no!" I called, feigning enormous distress.

The youngsters collected all the markers and returned them to their basket, and I reclaimed my seat at the front of the room.

"Hmm, so now I have to think of something that has happened to me. It doesn't need to be something big—like a birthday party or a vacation. Instead, I want to think about a *Small* Moment story. Hmm, I know! I could write about how I went running this morning and ran through a puddle and mud splashed on my leg. That would be a great story. *Or* I could write

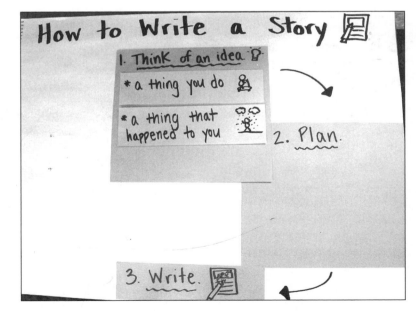

FIG. 1–1 "How to Write a Story" chart

about how I burnt my English muffin this morning but scraped the burnt part into the trash. *Or* . . . what other small moment could I write about? I know! I could write about the moment that just happened right here, when I was carrying the basket of markers back to my seat and they spilled all over you!"

Recruit the children's help in thinking through how the incident might be told across the pages of a booklet.

"Help me think about how that story would go." Holding up my booklet and pointing to page 1, I said, "We'd need to think what happened first. Are you thinking of the picture I'd draw and the words I could write on the first page?" Turning to the second page, I said, "Then, we'd need to tell what happened next," and I pointed to the children who'd had markers rain down on them, to the scene of the action. "And then, I'd write about what happened finally," and I gestured to suggest that page might tell about how I'd returned to my seat. I didn't actually draw or write, to save time.

ACTIVE ENGAGEMENT

Channel children to think of and share a small moment, drawing from things they have done.

"Right now, will you all think about a small moment that happened to you? It could be something you did this morning before coming to school. Or just the other day. Don't think of a big, huge story like going on a vacation, but instead, think of a small moment, like the time your grandma put barrettes in your hair or the time you fell out of bed."

"Thumbs up if you've thought of a time." Many children signaled they had, and I said, "Turn and tell someone near you the true story that is coming to your mind. Tell them the whole story, like we just told the story of the markers spilling. Tell what you did and said first, then next, and next. Go!"

The talk began quietly and then escalated as writers talked. For a minute, I crouched close to one writer and then another, listening to stories of the lights going out in the storm, finding a dollar bill in the couch, spilling milk at breakfast, going to the park and then seeing a friend from school, losing a tooth and putting it under the pillow.

Debrief in a way that sets up writers to think in similar ways any time they are searching for an idea for a story.

"Writers, today you are going to have a chance to write your own story, like George McClements has done. I hope you have learned that to write a story, you think about things you have done, things that happened to you, and then you pick one story and remember what happened first, then next and next so that you can write the story across pages."

At this point in the year your students will be writing across three-page booklets. As your students write more elaborate stories, they will write across more pages. This is why it is important to have single pages and a stapler available in the writing center so they can add mores pages.

Asking children to focus on a small moment immediately, even as they choose what to write about, will significantly improve the quality of their writing. This will help children steer clear of writing that starts at sunrise and ends with bed, with lists of activities in between.

If the children are having a hard time coming up with story ideas, still resist giving them topics. Sure, share the kinds of topics they might choose, Small Moment stories, but leave the choice to them. How to choose a topic is something writers must learn, even small writers.

LINK

Show a quick example of a finished book and then ask kids to recall a moment, think what happened first, and get started writing their stories across the pages of booklets.

"You'll see booklets in the trays on your table. You'll be writing true stories of one small moment that happened to you. Giancarlo, the first-grader who lives near me, wrote a story the other day. Do you want to hear it?" I read this to them. (See Figure 1–2.)

> Page 1: When I was riding my bike with my friends I fell down. I started to cry.
> Page 2: It hurt very bad VERY bad! I had to get a bandage.
> Page 3: My mommy took me inside. I watched some TV. And I said, "Cool!"

"Before you get started, think to yourself, 'What is the one story I am going to write today?'" I left a little pool of silence. "Think of the picture you are going to make on the first page. What did you do first, or what happened first? When you have your first page in mind, give me a thumbs up."

As children put their thumbs up, I sent them off to get started.

FIG. 1–2   Giancarlo's story about falling off his bike, which is an example of the level of writing first-graders often produce during the first part of the Small Moment unit

Channeling Children toward Writing Productively

SOME OF THE MOST IMPORTANT TEACHING YOU DO during a writing workshop will occur in the one-to-one conferences and in the small groups you lead as children write. This section of the book will generally help you make maximum use of those interactions. But for now, it is unlikely that your kids will be able to carry on with enough independence for you to linger for a few minutes in these conversations. Instead, you will probably need to put on your roller skates and move quickly from one corner of the room to another, making sure your physical presence is felt by all the children. So today our goal is to help you use a variety of methods to keep all your children working for as long as possible.

Your gestures alone can have a big effect. As soon as you send children off to work, try traveling quickly among all the writers, using gestures to channel as many kids as possible toward their work. If you see one child who has begun work especially early, give that child a thumbs-up signal. Others will see your gesture of support and turn to their pages, intent on earning similar recognition. Point to a child's words and say, "Yeah!"

Your gestures can not only celebrate; they can also direct. Tap on the page of a child's work, signaling, "Get started." Put a pen in yet another's hand. Make a "What gives?" shrug alongside the work area where two youngsters are squabbling over a marker pen.

You could also chronicle what children are doing, or what they should be doing, in voiceovers that you say loudly enough that they reach all the members of the class. "I love the way that Robert has gone from drawing to writing. He's saying his words slowly, listening to the sounds and getting them down. Wow, Robert!" A bit later, "Writers, do you remember how George McClements put details in his story? Well, Sophia's got similar details in her story! Listen to this one."

As you move, you may find that so many children need essential help that you decide to convene a whole table full of children. You can decide, for example, to check on

MID-WORKSHOP TEACHING
Writers Do the Best They Can and Move On

"Writers, eyes here, please." Once everyone had paused and looked up, I said, "I love your courage. When you aren't sure how to spell, you aren't acting like a scaredy-cat." I role-played a scaredy-cat by putting my fingernails in my mouth and shivering with fright. "No way! You just say," and I changed my posture to that of confidence, "'I'll do the best I can and keep going.' And when you aren't sure how to draw something, you don't say, 'Oh, no! Help me! I can't make a bicycle. I can't make my grandma's hat. I'm so scared. I can't draw it right.' No way! Instead you say," and this time they chimed in, "I'll do the best I can and keep going!"

"Show the person near you a place in your writing where you did something brave. It might have been a hard drawing or a hard word. Find a place where you could have said, 'No way. Help me, help me!' and where, instead, you said, 'I'll do the best I can and keep going.'"

As Students Continue Working . . .

"I love your stories! Liam's story is about how he showed his backpack to his friend on the school bus. Sarah is writing about how she lost a tooth when she bit into a cookie. These are great Small Moment stories!"

"Remember, writers, think what happened first and then next and next."

"Don't forget to stretch your words out the best you can, writing the sounds you hear."

"Brendan just did something really independent. He finished a story, and do you think he just sat there, saying, 'I'm done.' No way! Instead, he got *another* booklet from the writing center and started writing his *second* story! Wow, Brendan!"

whether everyone has gotten started drawing a story across the pages of a booklet, and when you find that some haven't yet done that, you can gesture to them, saying, "Come with me." Then, once you have a cluster of children pulled together in a huddle on the floor, you can repeat the directions for that day, using the work of one child as an exemplar to clarify what you hope all of them are doing.

You may use a similar method to teach groups of children some of the ways to make their writing even better. For example, you may pull together a few youngsters who could benefit from coaching that helps them add details to their drawings. If their characters are floating, then it helps to ground them. You might teach these children to ask themselves, "Where was I?" Once that answer is voiced, the writer can notice that the text—the drawing—just shows a person, floating in air. Usually authors not only show the person, but also show the place. If a group of children add the ground to all the pages of their booklet that may not seem like a big deal, but actually, the appearance of a ground line marks a big step ahead in children's drawing and makes it more likely that the characters will interact with each other, making the story more complex.

You will also want to channel children to write words to accompany their drawings. Most children will come into first grade reading at level C or D, and as such, you should expect that they can write words that contain beginning, middle, and ending sounds. If the child hasn't written any words, start with labels. "Who is that?" you ask, and when the child says, "Me," say, "Write that, then, so readers will know." Then fix your eyes on the paper, not noticing if the child looks into your eyes with that pleading "Help"

look. Tap the page. "Just put it right here," you can say, fully confident the child can write *me*. Most first-graders can do this, but whatever the child does, this will show you what she can do and allow you to adapt your teaching. Once you've coached the child to label and she has produced at least an initial letter, channel the writer to write a sentence caption under the picture as well. If a child wants *you* to draw or write for her, resist creating that sort of a dependency. With all the lightness and confidence in the world, you'll seize that request as an invitation to support approximation. "Oh my goodness, you wouldn't want *my* writing on your paper. Tell me what this is that you have drawn? Oh! Cool! So, just write that right here. Just write it as best you can." Then if the child writes something that looks like chicken scratch, "Look, you wrote it! Where else do you want to put some writing?"

After twenty minutes, the room may begin to unravel. You'll rely on mid-workshop teaching points as a support structure for keeping writers working. Early in the year, these interludes function as stones across the river, helping the students last throughout the entire workshop. It is not uncommon to have several mid-workshop teaching points in a day's writing workshop, especially during these first days. It is also entirely possible that the writing workshop will be abbreviated for this first week. Because you have not yet had a chance to teach writers to carry on with any independence, to go from one piece of writing to another, to add details to their drawings, to spell as best they can, or any of those other lessons, your children may not yet know how to sustain themselves, and so you'll stop while the going is good, shifting to a share meeting once many children seem to be at loose ends.

Writing Small Moments Like Mentor Authors

Remind children they are aiming to write stories like those by the mentor author. Then list what that author have done—writing a Small Moment story sequentially, including details—and ask, "Did you do that?"

"Writers, will each of you write your name on your writing and then bring your stories and come back to our meeting area so that we can talk about the work you did today?" Once the children had gathered, I said, "I started our day by reading you *Night of the Veggie Monster*. I suggested that maybe, just maybe, you guys could write Small Moment stories like that book.

"George didn't write about a whole day, or even a whole evening, did he? He just wrote about a small moment that happened when the boy tasted a pea for the first time. Did any of you do the same thing—write not about a whole day but about a small moment? Thumbs up if you, like George, wrote about a small moment!

"I also noticed that George told what happened first (the boy puts the pea in his mouth and his eyes begin to water) and next (his toes twist and curl up and he squirms in his seat), telling the story in order. Did any of you do that—tell your story in order? Thumbs up if you did!

"George writes with details, too, doesn't he? He didn't say, 'I ate it.' He tells us exactly what he did when he put the pea in his mouth. 'My eyes begin to water. My toes twist and curl up in my shoes.' Did any of you do that—write with details? Thumbs up if you used details like George did! Wow!"

Channel writers to share with a classmate the stories they've written.

"I am so excited to see that many of you wrote a Small Moment story today! Please turn and share your story with the person next to you."

I waited a few minutes, listening in as the children read their stories to one another, and then, not waiting for them all to finish, called for their attention. "Writers, eyes up here. I am *definitely* going to have to read your stories tonight. They sound terrific! Pass them to me, and tomorrow I'll give them back."

Don't despair if few thumbs go up. This is of course not really a question, it is a reminder. Children will learn from it for their writing tomorrow . . . and beyond.

Not only will it be exciting to read about your new children's lives, this is, of course, also a key time to assess their writing work and process. You'll no doubt study their work and begin to understand where along progressions of development each child lies, and where they might take a next step.

Planning for Writing

Writers Touch and Tell, Sketch, Then Write

Y OU WILL HAVE READ THROUGH YOUR CHILDREN'S WORK and, in your mind, you may have a long list of wishes for your kids. You may find yourself wishing that they would draw more representationally, write actual sequential narratives—not just captions to drawings—spend less time drawing and more time writing, and write stories that unfold across pages instead of pile all on one page. You are wise to wish for these things, but it is premature to be discouraged. In the span of just a single week, children's writing will improve dramatically. A week from now, you and your students will be able to look back on the writing they did that first day of writing workshop and celebrate growth. So convey to the children that they are off to an exciting start and that, over the course of just the next few days, their writing is going to change in ways that will knock everyone's socks off.

Of course, your challenge will then be to make sure this learning curve actually gets underway. This session contributes to that. Many experienced first-grade teachers regard this as one of the most essential minilessons of all, which is why it is so prominently placed within this unit. You will be teaching students how to plan for writing in a way that makes their stories far more coherent. By teaching them to say their entire story aloud before starting to draw, you make it less likely that children will sit in front of the page, thinking, "What do I know how to draw?" and then draw that item—a house with a picket fence, a horse, some tulips, a spacecraft. Today's instruction helps them start with a story line, which supports the important work they are learning to do in first grade as they work toward meeting the Common Core Narrative Writing Standards (in which they are expected to recount two or more appropriately sequenced events, include some details regarding what happened, use temporal words to signal event order, and provide some sense of closure). It gives them a chance to use the story language they learned in kindergarten—"One day . . . then . . . after that . . . "—that you'll want to encourage them to use when telling stories *and* writing stories. This oral rehearsal also helps them think of an entire story, envisioning that story as a whole. This makes it much more likely that they'll produce a story that has a beginning, a middle, and an end. As you'll see in upcoming sessions, the fact that

IN THIS SESSION, you'll teach children that writers plan what they want to write about before they start writing.

GETTING READY

✔ Booklets students wrote in Session 1, to be placed on their tables. Blank booklets for each student, to be distributed in the meeting area before the lesson begins.

✔ Writing folders for each student, with two pockets for storing writing pieces. You might want to label the pockets so that students put completed work on one side (using a red dot) and ongoing writing on the other (using a green dot) (see Share). You can store the folders in bins, one bin for each table, and set these out at the start of the share.

✔ Writing toolboxes on each table. After today, you will have table monitors set out their table's toolboxes and writing folder bins before the minilesson begins. All materials will be stored at the writing center.

✔ "How to Write a Story" chart, to be added to during the Connection

✔ Blank booklet made of chart paper for demonstrating different problems students had with their writing and for filling in with a new story (see Connection)

✔ Sample Small Moment story to demonstrate with, ideally the same one you planned out in Session 1 (see Connection and Share)

✔ Narrative Writing Checklist, Grades K and 1 (see Share)

COMMON CORE STATE STANDARDS: W.1.3, W.1.5; RL.1.7, RFS.1.1, RFS.1.2, RFS.1.3; SL.1.1, SL.1.4, SL.1.5; L.1.1, L.1.2

children go from saying the story to drawing it ends up helping them orient themselves so that if they start and stop writing midway, they can recall what they have written and what they plan to write next. This becomes especially important when their work spans several days.

"Oral rehearsal helps children think of an entire story, envisioning that story as a whole."

It is important to note that you will not be providing writers with a strategy for generating narrative writing until the very end of the day, in the share session. This means today's instruction will move children away from a reliance on you and the minilesson for help generating story ideas. The minilesson requires that children rely on the strategies they learned the day before (think of what you do or think of things that happen to you) to come up with an idea for a true story, so you'll want to make the "How to Write a Story" chart visible for the children to refer to easily. It is only the second day of your workshop, then, and already you are expecting writers to bring what they have learned one day to the next, drawing on all they know to write as well as possible.

Planning for Writing
Writers Touch and Tell, Sketch, Then Write

CONNECTION

Tell children that you read and appreciated their stories, but also point out some challenges you are seeing, like sometimes they wrote the whole story on one page or jumped from one story to another.

"Writers, last night, instead of taking my chapter book to bed and reading that before I went to sleep, I took your writing to bed with me. As I read what you wrote, I learned that you all have so many interesting small moments. Did you know that Ronald once held a starfish at the aquarium and that George built a snowman with his dad last winter and then they put a hat on it?

"It seemed, from what I read, that most of you didn't have any trouble coming up with ideas for true stories, and that is really great. You already know the first step to writing a story." I brought out the chart that was started the day before.

"Sometimes, though, it seemed that putting your story across *all* the pages of your booklet was a little hard for you. Some of you wrote your story all on one page, like this." I held up a blank booklet and said the words aloud as I touched the page.

"Page 1: Talking all in a rush, I blurted this out.

> One day, I forgot to bring the markers to the meeting area. So during the minilesson, I walked across the meeting area, got the basket full of markers, and started back to my chair. Then I spilled the markers all over the kids. Then the kids put them back in the basket and I went back to my chair.

"Page 2: nothing. Page 3: nothing.

"And some of you wrote your books like this. Page 1: The story about one small moment, like when I spilled the markers. Page 2: The story of a whole different time, like when I saw a woodpecker.

Remember to celebrate the writing and the work children have done—for this first story, you are their audience and they are no doubt hungry for a response! You will want to be sure they understand from you that their strengths as writers lead you to offer them teaching to help them grow even stronger.

Of course, if you found different, more pressing issues in their stories, you'll need to bring those to their attention. Over the years and across many, many classrooms, these are the needs we've usually encountered at this point in the unit.

"I'm not surprised it was hard to stretch your story across your pages, because I never taught you the trick that kids across the whole world use to plan their stories. You ready to learn this trick?"

❖ Name the teaching point.

"Today I want to teach you that after young writers come up with an idea for their stories, they plan by doing this: touch and tell, sketch, then write. Instead of getting a booklet and then starting to draw page 1, they touch and tell, sketch, *then* write."

I revealed the process chart and pointed to the strategies of "touch and tell, then sketch across pages." Then I pointed to step 3: Write!

It helps to provide visual support by gesturing in sync with your teaching point. You can touch the page, then make a speech bubble with your hands when you say "tell," and then pantomime sketching. If you do those same action each time you say this and say the sequence of actions like a chant, with the same intonation, children will soon "sing along."

How to Write a Story

1. THINK OF AN IDEA.

   - a thing that happened to you
   - a thing you do

2. PLAN.

   - touch and tell, then sketch across pages

3. WRITE!

TEACHING

Tell children that writers rein themselves in from starting writing without planning. Demonstrate steps for preparing to write by doing so with the shared class story from the previous day.

"Many writers—grown-up writers and young writers, both—get so excited to write that they start writing without thinking about how the story will go, and that's when they end up writing the whole story on one page or forgetting important parts of the story or sometimes even writing a whole *other* story in the same book! So writers have learned that it really helps to get ready to write. After they think of an idea, they plan how their stories will go.

"Maybe you can help me get ready to write, following our planning steps—touch and tell, sketch, *then* write—and then you'll have a chance to plan too.

"Writers, we never did make a book out of the spilled markers, so let's do it now." I picked up the marker and looked as if I was about to draw a picture on page 1. "I better draw me, walking over to the markers," I muttered, as if to myself, and then stopped myself before starting the picture.

"Oh, I have to remember to get ready to write before I draw my picture!" I looked at the chart to remind myself to plan. "Hmm, touch and tell the story. To do this, I need to remember where I was and what was happening." I touched the first page.

> One day, I forgot to bring the markers to the meeting area. So during the minilesson, I walked across the meeting area, got the basket full of markers, and started back to my chair.

ACTIVE ENGAGEMENT

Recruit students to touch and tell the upcoming pages in the shared class story.

I again started to draw on that page and again corrected myself, saying, "I better touch and tell across *all* of my pages. I'll start at the beginning, and then will you help by touching and telling the rest of the pages? Pretend this is your story and that you have an invisible booklet in front of you, and touch and tell the upcoming pages. You'll need to describe those markers coming raining down on some of you. You can use words like *then* or *after that* to get you started saying how the next page will go." I reread the story up to that point.

As the children continued the story, I listened in for a few seconds and then touched and told a version of the final pages of the story, created from listening to what the children were saying.

> While walking across the rug to my chair, I dropped the whole basket of markers. They fell everywhere.
> After that we put them back in the basket, and I went back to my chair.

Rally students to sketch with invisible pens the first page of the shared story.

"Hmm, now that I have touched and told the story, what do we do next?" I gestured toward the chart, and the children called out that we needed to sketch and then write the story. I turned back to page 1 and this time muttered to myself, "Let's see, what happened on the first page? Oh, yes, that's when I got the markers. I'll sketch that quickly. I better just draw what is important—me, you guys, the basket of markers. Got it." Then I turned the page.

"This will be the main part of the story, right? When those markers came flying down at you guys! Before we write, we need to sketch this page, too. Try it, quickly. Make a picture in your mind of the basket falling and then markers raining down all over you guys, and with your invisible pen and your invisible booklet, sketch that picture." As children worked, I coached, "This is just a sketch, so it should be the outlines, and you need to work quickly."

You may demonstrate writing in front of the class using chart paper and a marker so that your text is visible to all students. The children, however, will write with pencils or pens.

This teaching and active engagement are a bit different than usual in that there is more back-and-forth between teacher and children. Here, we have asked children to try something, step by step, offering coaching along the way. This kind of scaffolding is often unnecessary, but in introducing this new, multistep process, it is a helpful way to teach. Here, it goes like this: I show, they try; I show something else, they try that something else.

After a minute, I said, "Turn the page of your invisible booklet and tell the person beside you what we'll need to sketch on page 3 *and* what we need to do after we sketch page 3. Go!"

The children talked to each other, and I checked in, listening. This took just a minute—no longer. Not waiting for them to be done, I said, "So I hear you saying we need to finish sketching page 3, and then we can get started writing the story, starting with, 'One day, I forgot to bring the markers to the meeting area.'"

Debrief, noting the way the class has touched and told, then sketched and written. Rally the children to chant, "Writers touch and tell, sketch, then write."

"Writers, did you see how we didn't just start writing words right away? We had our story idea, and we got ready to write. We touched each page and told the story, then we sketched on each page, and now we are ready to write the words. Say it with me." Then the children chimed in, and we chanted, "Writers touch and tell, sketch, then write." I added, "One more time," and again, the class chanted, "Writers touch and tell, sketch, then write!"

LINK

Channel writers to think of the story they will write and to prepare to write that story by planning across pages.

"Writers you each have a blank booklet under your legs. This is so you can practice getting ready for writing the story you will write today or another day. So, first, think of an idea." I pointed to "Think of an idea" on the process chart. "Give me a thumbs up when you have something in your mind."

Once thumbs went up, I said, "Now, take your booklets out from under your legs, look at the first page, and let's plan. Touch that page, thinking about where you were at the start of the story and what you were doing. Tell the story you will write on that page. You might start by saying, 'One day. . . .'"

After children touched and told their first page, I said, "Okay, now turn to the next page, and the next, touching and telling the story on each page. When you turn the page you might say 'then' or 'after that' since you are moving to the next part of the story." As children finished page 2, I gestured for them to move on to tell page 3. "What's next? Touch and tell . . . "

The children called, "Sketch," and I said, "With your imaginary pen, sketch what you'd put on the first page, then the second." In no time, I added, "Soon, writers, you will be doing our last step—writing the words! That is the best step of all. Who is ready to go back to your seat and touch and tell and sketch the book you are working on from yesterday's workshop or start a new book like this one you just planned here in the meeting area?"

The pace of all this is incredibly important. You can't wait for every child to complete each step of the process, or the whole class will spend huge amounts of time waiting. The children who finish quickly will get restless, plus the entire process will feel like a prolonged one. Move this along by giving just a few seconds for each step. Don't for a moment think this is about waiting until everyone is done and all eyes are on you before moving to another step.

We don't always ask children to get started writing while they are still in the meeting area. This does work well, though, on days when you anticipate it's harder to get started than usual. Human nature is to avoid work that is abstract or daunting, and getting started can dispel both of those impressions of writing.

Support Independence So that You Can Teach

DURING THIS SECOND DAY OF YOUR WRITING WORKSHOP, you'll find that, once again, you need to move briskly among your students. As you do this, keep in mind that one of the most important things you are teaching right now is independence. If your messages are clear, you'll soon have a class of students that can carry on, working productively for half an hour, without needing you to do very much maintenance. It is essential that you teach writers to be resourceful problem solvers, because until they can do this, it will be hard for you to lead the small groups and the one-to-one conferences that are essential to your children's growth.

You can only support independence if you allow yourself to be comfortable with approximation. You will see children doing lots of things that are not perfect, and if you stay with one child and then another, working zealously to transform that child's work or process into something marvelous, you are apt to do so at the cost of keeping everyone working productively. So for now, tell yourself that the first goal is for children to be confident writers, able to come up with ideas for writing, to start a story, to rehearse it, to write it, and to move to another. It is not a priority, just yet, for a child to spell every sight word correctly or to write perfectly focused stories.

If a child comes to you to say, "I finished. What should I do now?" instead of acting as if it is the most natural thing in the world for the writer to expect you to give marching orders, signal that it won't be the norm for the child to come to you at each step of his or her work. Ask, with surprise, "So why did you come to me? Do you know what writers do when they finish one story?" If the child answers, "They write another?" support that response. As the youngster skips off, add, "And next time when you are done, you don't need to come to me to ask what to do next. You are the boss of your own writing!" This may sound tough, but you can say all this with affection, and unless you are decisive and clear, children will continue to lean on you for every last thing.

If you support independence, this will allow you to teach. Instead of doling out paper, sharpening pencils, collecting finished work, and initiating next steps, you want to actually teach. If you are lucky, even today, you'll have some chances to do that. When

---

MID-WORKSHOP TEACHING   Sketches Help Writers Remember What They Were Going to Write

"Writers, can I stop you? All eyes up here. Earlier today, you learned to plan your stories by touching and telling the story across pages and then sketching across pages.

"If you did that work before writing a story today, put your thumbs up." Most indicated they had done this. "And if you finish your story right about now and go to start another story, tell the person near you what you will do after you think of an idea for that *next* story." The children gestured to the "How to Write a Story" chart and repeated the mantra: "touch and tell, sketch, *then* write."

"Writers, there is another reason why this strategy works. Sometimes, you look away from your writing—like you have been doing right now to listen to me. And when you look back at your writing, you can forget what you were going to say! You start back at the beginning of your story and touch and tell, but this time you are reading, right? Then you get to the sketch you were just in the middle of drawing, look at it—and finish it!"

The children gestured toward the chart, and I agreed. "Try it now. You've been away from your writing. Reread your story to the person sitting next to you, and when you get to a part without words, use the sketch to help you remember what to write next. Say what you'll write, and then write it!"

Children did this, and then as they restarted their writing, I voiced over, saying "See how those sketches helped you remember your stories? Keep writing."

---

you confer or lead small groups, you will certainly want to reinforce today's lesson, because it is essential for writers to get into the habit of "writing-in-the-air" as a way to rehearse for writing. To teach, however, you need to understand children's needs. Sometimes children who are not touching and telling across pages will be struggling not with the planning strategy you just taught, but with coming up with story ideas in the first place. If there are a number of children who need help with this, gather them into a quick huddle and say, "I called you here because I saw you were stuck on what to write about. Remember that yesterday, we realized that if you are stuck on a story idea, it helps to think, 'What are some things that I do?' So right now, think: what are some things that you do a lot? For example, I go running a lot, and I feed my dogs a lot. What do you do a lot?" When children produce answers like "Ride the bus?" "Play at recess?" nod and say, "Yes! Terrific! So think of one particular time you did that—one time you rode the bus, one time you played at recess." Then leave a pool of silence. "You got an idea?" By then, most of the children should be set, and you can work one on one to support any child needing that support.

You will also want to use your teaching time to help children go from drawing to writing. "Tell me your story," you can say, and then when the child says the sentence that belongs on page 1, say that sentence back to her. Sometimes I alter the wording just a bit to make the writing easier. So when a child says, "I was riding my bike," I might say, "So write that: 'I rode my bike.'" If the child looks at me blankly, I'd be apt to say, "Let's say the words and touch the paper where you'll write them. I'll show you." To demonstrate, I might dictate the words as I move my finger along the page, and then I'd say, "You try it." After the child says the words she will write, touching the place where each word will go, I bring her back to say the first word, which in this instance is *I*. After she writes that, I'd probably say, "Okay, so read what you have written, touching it, and keep going."

Setting Up for Ongoing Writing

Celebrate the volume of story-making by giving children folders for storing work.

While children were still writing at their tables, I said, "Oh my goodness, it's like a story factory in here. This process—touch and tell, sketch, then write—sure got you guys to write a lot of stories! You have so many stories now that you need a special container for storing them, so I'm going to give each of you a folder for your writing. I've put a red dot on one pocket of your folder, for work that is stopped, and a green dot on the other side of your folder, for work that

Narrative Writing Checklist

	Kindergarten	NOT YET	STARTING TO	YES!	Grade 1	NOT YET	STARTING TO	YES!
	Structure				**Structure**			
Overall	I told, drew, and wrote a whole story.	☐	☐	☐	I wrote about when I did something.	☐	☐	☐
Lead	I had a page that showed what happened first.	☐	☐	☐	I tried to make a beginning for my story.	☐	☐	☐
Transitions	I put my pages in order.	☐	☐	☐	I put my pages in order. I used words such as *and* and *then, so*.	☐	☐	☐
Ending	I had a page that showed what happened last in my story.	☐	☐	☐	I found a way to end my story.	☐	☐	☐
Organization	My story had a page for the beginning, a page for the middle, and a page for the end.	☐	☐	☐	I wrote my story across three or more pages.	☐	☐	☐
	Development				**Development**			
Elaboration	My story indicated who was there, what they did, and how the characters felt.	☐	☐	☐	I put the picture from my mind onto the page. I had details in pictures and words.	☐	☐	☐
Craft	I drew and wrote some details about what happened.	☐	☐	☐	I used labels and words to give details.	☐	☐	☐
	Language Conventions				**Language Conventions**			
Spelling	I could read my writing.	☐	☐	☐	I used all I knew about words and chunks of words (*at, op, it,* etc.) to help me spell.	☐	☐	☐
	I wrote a letter for the sounds I heard.	☐	☐	☐	I spelled all the word wall words right and used the word wall to help me spell other words.	☐	☐	☐
	I used the word wall to help me spell.	☐	☐	☐				

You'll want to keep the Narrative Writing Checklist, Grade K with you as you confer over the next several days, and look ahead to the Grade 1 Checklist. You can use both to point out things that children are doing well and also areas of potential growth—writing goals.

Of course, the share that I've written is just one possibility. You could, instead, simply say to the class, "When I point to you, will you stand up and tell all of us—using just one word— what you wrote about?" "Hold up your beautiful writing! Oh look, I notice that . . . and I notice that. . . ."

"Wow! I learned so much about each of you today. I learned that Josh loves his family picnics because he wrote about it. Skylah loves to ice-skate, and Brendan is crazy about his dog. I know all these things because these writers wrote about them. From now on, we are going to live like writers who write about things they are very passionate about, that they are crazy about! Great writing, writers!"

is still going, stories you aren't finished with. It is just like how we stop at a red light and keep going at a green light. Right now, find your writing folder in the special bin on your table, date your work with the date stamp, and then slide your work carefully (so it doesn't bunch up) into the pocket with the red dot."

Introduce writers to other systems for organizing materials and the role of table monitors.

"Writers, I've listed this week's table monitors up here." I gestured to a list of one name from each table. "Table monitors help us keep our materials organized, making sure our folders, pencils, and other writing tools are kept neat and safe in our toolboxes, and they store all this in the writing center. Right now, writers, make sure your folders are in the folder bin and the pencils, pens, and date stamp are back in the toolbox. Table monitors, take the bins and toolboxes to the writing center. You will set up your tables with these materials tomorrow before writing workshop begins."

End by asking writers to reflect on the narrative writing goals they worked on last year, rallying them for the work of setting new goals this year.

"And writers," I said after calling the children back to the meeting area, "I have one last thing I want to share with you." I pointed to the Narrative Writing Checklist, Grades K and 1, displayed in the meeting area. "It is the checklist you used last year to set goals and reflect on the progress you made as narrative writers." I pointed to the Grade K Checklist. "I know many of you remember these goals from last year and have already been doing them in your writing this year. In a moment, I'm going to read each item on the list. As I read, thumbs up if you are already doing this in your stories. If not, that's okay. Those are the goals you can keep working at. Soon, though, you'll be working off of a new checklist that has the goals you should be working toward as first-grade narrative writers, so I've included that checklist next to the kindergarten one. Remember, writers improve when they reflect on where they are and set goals to try new things in their writing."

You may want to send the folders home or give students an opportunity to bring in photographs, magazine clippings, or drawings that remind them of moments in their lives. In this way, the folders provide writers with a tool for generating ideas.

FIG. 2–1   These folders have a plastic sleeve on the front so that students were able to decorate a blank piece of white paper with pictures. The decorated papers easily slid into the plastic sleeves.

Using Pictures to Add On

IN MOST PRIMARY UNITS OF STUDY, by the second or third day, you'll probably want to teach a minilesson that supports revision. This is necessary because young kids (and actually, perhaps all of us) have a tendency to whip through things quickly. It is not uncommon for first-graders to generate a story a day, or even two stories a day, with each story containing no more than a one-sentence caption on each page. First-grade teachers will often find that they no sooner send all the children off to get started than one child will pop up to say, "I'm done." Soon another pops up as well. That refrain, "I'm done! I'm done!" signals that it is time for you to remind children of that saying, "When you're done, you have just begun." Kindergarten teachers taught this to children as well, encouraging them to go back and add more to their drawings and their words. Your children are first-graders now, so instead of encouraging them to add more detail to their drawings, you'll help them interrogate their drawings to get ideas for content they can add into the written text, adding details to strengthen writing as needed.

Over the course of this year, you'll be teaching all your students to write not just one-liners, but paragraphs. This means some children will be ready to be pushed toward paragraphs now, and if your school is one in which children have had many literacy opportunities prior to entering your classroom, you'll find that many of them are ready for this work. If children are writing either just labels on their pictures or just a single sentence at the bottom of a page, the first step toward getting them to write with more volume and elaboration is to teach them to return to work they thought was done and to consider adding yet more to it. As children learn to reread and revise by elaborating, they'll hopefully also learn that their writing can be written with more detail from the very start. Many of them have learned already to put the important details in their sketches—the people, the setting, the action. They are ready to include these details in their words. Today's session, then, is not just a lesson in revision. It is also a lesson in elaboration.

You'll be using the same piece of writing that you and the class generated when you spilled markers all over the class, creating the ground for a shared story. The wonderful thing about a story such as this is that although it is technically your piece of writing,

IN THIS SESSION, you'll teach children that writers use pictures to help them add words to tell their stories.

GETTING READY

✔ Your own writing folder containing the shared class story revised during yesterday's minilesson (see Teaching and Active Engagement)

✔ "How to Write a Story" chart, with new bullet (Revise) added (see Connection)

✔ Revision strips (two-, three-, and four-line strips cut from writing paper) for students to use as they revise their stories. They can write their revisions on the strips and then add them to the middle or ends of their pages. They can tape the strip onto the part where the new words fit and leave it there as a flap of paper that can be lifted up to reveal the words written beneath. Add these revision strips (and tape) to each writing toolbox. (see Share)

COMMON CORE STATE STANDARDS: W.1.3, W.2.3, W.1.5; RL.1.7; SL.1.1, SL.1.2, SL.1.5; L.1.1, L.1.2

it is also the class's piece of writing. The children can add their own two cents about the details you should include. This allows you to demonstrate in ways that draw kids in as participants. "Help me do this," you say, and you get children thinking alongside you about the details that can be added to the story. Always, demonstrations are most effective when there is a thin line between the teacher demonstrating and the learner attempting that same thing. You saw that thin line between demonstration and active engagement when this class story was conceived and planned, and you'll see it again in this session.

"Today's session is not just a lesson in revision. It is also a lesson in elaboration."

Of course, when you ask children to be actively involved in today's minilesson, the real goal is not their engagement with whole-class instruction, though this is no small feat. Instead, the real goal is their engagement with revision. It will be an accomplishment if you can draw children toward an acceptance of revision as an essential part of the writing process. A first step will be for you to be clear that revision is *not* too hard for young kids! In science education, you learn that the scientific method is something that even five-year-olds can experience. And they do, working to explore which objects float and which sink in water. In the same way, your six-year-olds can participate in the writing process. Their revisions will be very concrete, involving flaps for additional text. Young children find revision to be totally natural, if you teach it as such. Thus far this year, your children have learned to rehearse and draft. Today, they learn, also, to revise.

Using Pictures to Add On

CONNECTION

As a prelude to your teaching point, re-create thinking that you are done with earlier writing about a shared incident and then realizing that the story is too short.

"Writers, when you come to the meeting area, please bring your folder of writing with you and sit on it," I said, and then waited until the class had assembled on the carpet. "The other day, you and I planned a story about the time I spilled the markers all over your heads. You'll remember the story went like this."

> One day, I forgot to bring the markers to the meeting area. So during the minilesson, I walked across the meeting area, got the basket full of markers, and started back to my chair.
> While walking across the rug to my chair, I dropped the whole basket of markers. They fell everywhere.
> After that we put them back in the basket, and I went back to my chair.

"Like you, I have a folder," I said, holding it up for everyone to see, "with a sticker on one pocket that signals 'finished work' and a sticker on the other pocket that signals 'ongoing work.' Yesterday I finished the story about spilling the markers, so I put it in my finished pocket. But I got to school early this morning, and I was looking for a good read-aloud book, and I thought, 'Would that story be a good read-aloud?' So I pulled that story out of the folder and reread it, and this time, you know what I thought? I thought, 'It's awfully short.' I mean, if I was to read my marker story aloud to you during story time, I'd open it up, start reading, and in a flash, I'd say, 'The end.' You'd all protest, 'That's it? That's our story for the day?'

"So I realized I better add a whole lot more to that story. And the same might be true for some of your stories. So right now, get a story out of *your* finished work pocket, and talk to the person beside you about whether your story might be awfully short, as well."

For a minute, the children pulled stories from their folders and shared them with each other. As Liam looked over his story about a funny clown at a party, he hit his head with his hand and said, "I'm so silly. I am not *done* with this story!" Then he added, "I forgot to say how the clown made me a monkey balloon at the party."

In this connection, I re-created a situation writers will find themselves in—a predictable problem writers have. This is an important part of teaching! If a writer doesn't recognize trouble, doesn't recognize the need for a certain writing tool or a certain writing strategy, then that tool or strategy is useless.

❖ Name the teaching point.

"Today I want to teach you that writers have a saying: 'When you're done, you've just begun.' Writers finish a piece and then go back and revise by adding more. They often look at the pictures (and make pictures in their mind by remembering the event) and think, 'Who? Where? When? What? How?' Writers make sure the answers to these questions are in their stories."

I'd written these questions on the process chart under 'Revise' so they'll always know where to look for them. Now I gestured toward the list as I spoke.

TEACHING

Playact thinking that your writing is done. When children protest, ask them to help you reread and revise.

"So, as I was saying, we wrote that story about the spilled markers, and it's all done. So I guess now what I'll do is put my feet up and eat pretzels." I leaned back, made an exaggerated stretching motion, and put my feet up. "All done."

The children, of course, protested. With feigned astonishment, I heard their calls of, "You gotta add on," and then, persuaded, put my feet down and agreed with them. "You are right. Writers have a saying: 'When you're done, you've just begun.'

"So, writers, would you help me look back at this story and see if we can come up with things to add? Let's try to add to the last two pages because they are soooo short. So, let's see, what does a writer do if she wants to revise, to add on?" I left a little pool of silence, in hopes children would recall the teaching point. "Oh yes, I remember! We look back at the picture, remember that time, and ask those questions." I gestured to where I'd written 'Who? Where? When? What? How?' Then I read page 2 aloud:

> While walking across the rug to my chair, I dropped the whole basket of markers. They fell everywhere.

"Let's look at the picture first and remember what happened." I stared at the drawing. "Hmm, I dropped the whole basket of markers. On who? Where? How?" Then I turned to the kids. "You remember that time, don't you? I was walking like this." I got out of my chair and physically re-created the journey I'd taken. "And then I dropped the markers. On who? Where? How?"

The kids were all on their knees, hands waving, eager to fill in the details for me. "You dropped them on *my* head," Brendan volunteered. "And all over me," Liam added. Emma, climbing onto her knees, piped in to say, "They were all over the place like crazy. Like, like, those pick-up sticks." Picking up my marker, I added another few sentences.

How to Write a Story

1. THINK OF AN IDEA.

   - a thing that happened to you
   - a thing you do

2. PLAN.

   touch and tell, then sketch across pages

3. WRITE!

4. REVISE.

   Who? Where? When? What? How?

You'll see that even though this is a demonstration and even though it is in the teaching section of the minilesson, not the active engagement section, the children are involved. Unless a learner can picture himself in the shoes of the demonstrator, doing the steps the demonstrator is doing, the teaching is apt to be weak.

Even though I don't explicitly state that physically reenacting a story can help writers revise, some children will be ready to take in this tucked-in tip. Tucking in tips like this is one way to differentiate your whole-class instruction. This can make further teaching and coaching available to those students who are ready for it.

While walking across the rug to my chair, I dropped the whole basket of markers. They fell every-where. They fell on Brendan's head, and they fell all over Liam. They splashed out all over the rug. They looked like a million pick-up sticks.

ACTIVE ENGAGEMENT

Recruit children to reread and revise the next page of the shared story.

"So we added onto page 2, didn't we! Can you guys see if *you* can revise the last page of this booklet?" I read it aloud.

After that we put them back in the basket, and I went back to my chair.

"Try this same strategy of looking at the picture to think up more stuff to say, and ask questions like 'Who? Where? When? What? How?'" Then I read the last page to the children and encouraged them to talk to each other.

After listening a bit to the hubbub, I called on Maxwell, who said, "We got them off the floor and we put 'em, we scooped them, into the basket, all the kids did." Cooper added, "It was a mountain of markers." I assured the children I would add it to the enlarged story soon.

Debrief on what the students just did, emphasizing ways their work is transferable to another day and another text.

"Writers, did you see how you reread the story and thought about what else you could add by looking at the pictures and by asking, 'Who? Where? What? How?' Those questions will help you make a teeny tiny story into a book that we could read aloud during story time!"

LINK

Repeat the teaching point and channel students to draw on this instruction and on all they have been learning thus far this year to keep the story factory going.

"Writers, when it is time to get to work, writers remember everything they know about writing. Thumbs up if today you will start a new story and will plan by touching and telling, sketching, then writing. Thumbs up if you are going to go back to a story that you thought was done and *add more* by looking at the picture and asking 'Who? Where? When? What? How?' Thumbs up if you will be working on something from the checklist you used last year and last workshop. Thumbs up if you have a different goal and plan. Okay! Off you go!"

Your most important job during the link is to restate the teaching point in a way that puts it into the context of children's ongoing writing work. But often you will do this by showing children that today's lesson adds to their growing repertoire of strategies.

Support Writers in Revising Finished Work and Rehearsing New Work

B Y NOW, THE CHILDREN IN YOUR CLASS will have been taught the entire personal narrative writing process. They know how to generate topics, to touch and tell the story they intend to write, to sketch, to write, and now to revise and elaborate as they reread the text and recall the experience, using their sketches as a scaffold. Expect that many of them will cycle through that entire process within a day, with a few who are writing several sentences a page spending longer on a single text.

Although conferences and small-group work do provide you with vehicles for ensuring that kids do the work of that day's minilesson, your teaching also needs to remind children to draw on the full repertoire of all they know how to do. It is helpful, then, to have the kindergarten and first-grade Continua for Narrative Writing with you as you confer, as a way to help writers set new goals for themselves and to monitor their progress in this genre. When conferring and leading small groups, you should also find that children pose challenges that require you to invent on your toes in response to what the children have done. This, then, allows you to use conferring and small-group work as a place where you can invent some new teaching ideas in response to the surprising challenges your kids are encountering.

On this particular day, you will probably need to remind some children that when they're done with a story, they won't immediately file it in the red-dot pocket of their folder and reach for a new booklet. Watch for kids who are en route to the paper supply. If you see someone starting a new piece, act as though you assume he or she has already produced vast amounts of revision. "How exciting!" you might say. "You have already added tons of things to your last story. Before you move to the next piece, can you walk me through your story and show me what you added?" Chances are that the youngster will not, in fact, have done any of the revisions you described during the minilesson. Act astonished. "*What?* You didn't do any revisions? That's what authors do!" Of course, you'll want to keep spirits high, so quickly add, "That's okay. We can do that work together. I *love* rereading and adding more."

For the reluctant reviser, you may start by encouraging revisions to the pictures. If the characters are floating, as is common, the child might add the setting, the ground, as this allows the picture to change from a list of components ("That's my mom.") to an interaction ("My mom is handing me the cookies."). Then too, the child might add

MID-WORKSHOP TEACHING
Using Strong Feelings to Generate Story Ideas

"Writers, can I stop you for a moment?" I waited until all eyes were on me. "Today Jazmin invented *another* strategy for coming up with great story ideas. Remember when we said that writers of true stories sometimes write about things that they do or things that happen to them? Well, Jazmin got the idea that she could write a story about a time when she had strong feelings. She wrote a story about a time when she was really scared. She was riding her bike, and everything was fine, and then her pant leg got twisted up in the bike and she started being a little worried, then it got worse and she was really scared. She fell off the bike onto the road.

"Talking about it afterward, Jazmin and I realized that whenever something happens that gives you a strong feeling, that is probably going to make a great story.

"Right now, think of one time when *you*, like Jazmin, were scared or had a different strong feeling." I left a pool of silence.

"Pretend you have a book in front of you and touch and tell the story of that one time to someone near you.

"Wow, writers, I heard some great stories about times when you had strong feelings. I even heard Emma tell a story about a time she was *brave*. So, writers, I've added Jazmin's strategy to our list of how writers of true stories get ideas. You can look at this list whenever you are stuck and don't have an idea for a story."

As Students Continue Working . . .

"Writers, I just saw Liam finish his story and start to get up for more paper, but then, guess what? He stopped! He sat back down in his chair, turned to his first page, and started rereading his story. He's acting like professional writers do!"

"Writers, right now, turn to a page of your story where you sketched a lot but didn't write too much. Point to one part of the sketch, tell the story of that part to yourself, in your mind, and then reread your words to see if you've written about that part of the picture. If not, do it now! Then keep doing this."

"Remember to keep looking back at your sketch. After you write the words for one page, look at the sketch again and think about what else you want to say. Write it. Then go back to the sketch one more time to see if there is anything else you can say!"

supplementary objects (the cookie, the dish, the nearby dog licking his lips) or capture actions in the drawings. The important thing will be to use the revisions to *sketches* as an engine for revisions to *writing*. You might harken back to yesterday's teaching and encourage children to reread the text they have written so far, to say the text they plan to add on, and then to begin recording those words.

Meanwhile, you'll also want to hold conferences in which you remind writers of everything you've taught so far this year. To do this, survey your classroom and decide on the biggest things that are getting in the way of children doing the work you have reinforced. Chances are that you will have some children who regard the writing workshop as art class. They work industriously to make delicate flowers on a dress and curtains in every window. Teach these youngsters that writers don't draw so much as they sketch. Session 8 contains a detailed focus lesson that can help you make this point. Other children's pictures may not be overly detailed, but they nevertheless still struggle with the transition between drawing and writing, recording very few words on the page. Chances are good that these are insecure spellers. You might convene a small group of these children and talk up the importance of spelling the best you can so you can keep going. You might coach this group to write faster, in unison. First remind them to look at a picture, to think what they are going to say, and then to touch and tell that page, saying aloud the words they plan to write. You might coach them to leave a little line on the page for each word they are about to write, and then to point to each line they've made, saying what they will write. "Now point to your first line and write that word. Say it once, say it slooowly, and then write it." Then channel the children to reread what they have written, touching the page, and when they have said their second word, to write it as well.

In this way, you'll provide the help to get all your children off the starting block.

Revising More with Revision Strips

Spotlight a conference in which you helped a child use revision strips to add on to his writing, and set other writers up to revise their stories in similar ways.

I convened the children into the meeting area and waited for them to give me their attention. "I was conferring with Maxwell today, and he wrote this wonderful story about going rock climbing." I read it aloud. (See Figure 3–1.)

> One summer I was at camp and I went rock climbing. It was so high.
> I got to the top.
> I came down and I bumped my head.

"He wanted to figure out what else he could add. He used the questions to help him check to see what details he already told the reader. Who was in the story? He was." I pointed to the Maxwell in the picture and the *I* in the words.

"Where? At camp." I pointed to the picture and the word *camp*.

"Then he thought to himself, 'When was it?' He realized he forgot to say *when* he was rock climbing. So here he added 'one summer' at the beginning. He used a caret—that's an upside down *v*—to insert those two words at the beginning of the sentence. Writers do that when they have just one or two words to add.

"Then Maxwell kept going. He asked himself, 'What was I doing?' 'Rock climbing.' He had that part in. I pointed to the picture and the words *rock climbing*.

"How? Then Maxwell said, 'How was I feeling? Oh, I was so scared!' he said. Then he went to add that in but couldn't fit it. He looked at me and said, 'But I don't have any more lines.'

"But do you think Maxwell just gave up? No way! Instead, he said, 'Wait! I can add more lines!' and he got a revision strip like this (one with two or three lines on it) and taped the paper onto where he wanted to write more words. Listen to how Maxwell's story sounds now." And I read the newly revised version.

Page 1: One Summer I was at kamp and I went rikliming. It was so hi. (ONE SUMMER I WAS AT CAMP AND I WENT ROCK CLIMBING. IT WAS SO HIGH.)

Added flap: I was so so sckard. (I WAS SO SO SCARED.)

"So, writers, from now on, you can borrow Maxwell's strategies of using a caret and adding lines onto your story when you have more to say and need more room. I put revision strips in your toolboxes along with tape so that when you need more lines you have them right there on your table.

"Let's try that right now. Reread one part of your story and then ask questions like Maxwell did to see if there is a detail missing that you could add." I pointed to the questions on the "How to Write a Story" chart. "Give me a thumbs up when you have something you can add." I waited until more than half of the thumbs were up. "Writers, turn to your partner and see if your partner has something to add." I listened in as writers shared. "I can add 'It was a hot summer day,'" said Jazmin. "I can add, 'I was in my bedroom' because that was where we played with my dolls," Sabrina said.

"Writers, if you are only adding one or two words, go ahead and use your pencil to add the caret and the words. If you need a revision strip, raise your hand and I'll pass that to you with a little piece of tape." Hands flew up, children eager to add more to their pages. I passed out the strips and everyone got to revising.

Debrief by reminding students they have the tools they need to revise any story they are writing.

"Writers, let's come back together. I saw some of you added a few words to your story with carets. A few of you added revision strips to the end of your page to add more words. I saw some of you add strips to the middle of the page because you realized you left something out in the middle of that part. Wow! Your writing toolboxes will have these tools so that you have them available whenever you reread your writing and realize you left something out.

"I want to remind you that we also have extra pages in the writing center in case you ever need to add a whole page inside your story *or* to the end of your story. Sometimes your story might be four or five pages long, and you can get up and staple the paper to your booklet. You can do this before you even start writing. When you plan, you might realize you need more pages. You can also do it once you've begun writing or finished writing and you realize you have more to say. I can't wait to see how you continue to revise your stories!"

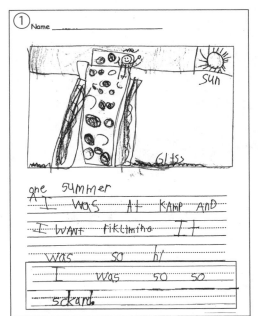

FIG. 3–1   Maxwell's rock-climbing story shows two types of revision as he used two words to tell where he was, using a caret, and then added how he was feeling, using a revision strip at the bottom of the first page.

Stretching Words to Spell Them

Hearing and Recording All Sounds

IN THIS SESSION, you'll teach children that writers spell by stretching out each word, listening for all the sounds and recording what they hear.

GETTING READY

✔ White board, marker, and eraser for each child. The minilesson will proceed more smoothly if children have used these tools in word study and interactive writing.

✔ Enlarged booklet, three pages long, on which you've already sketched and begun writing a story (see Teaching)

✔ An alphabet chart that is familiar to the children (from reading it during word study). Some, if not all, students may have these in their writing folders to reference during writing time. (see Teaching)

✔ A class name chart that was created on one of the first days of school during word study and that students can refer to when problem-solving words. Names are grouped by first letter and listed in alphabetical order. (see Active Engagement)

✔ Class word wall that has about five to ten words that have been added during word study. Many of these words are from kindergarten, and two or three have been introduced as ones the class is learning. (see Mid-Workshop Teaching)

✔ "Ways to Spell Words" chart, with first bullet prewritten, to be introduced during the Share

COMMON CORE STATE STANDARDS: W.1.3; RFS.1.2.c,d, RFS.1.3; SL.1.1; L.1.1, L.1.2.d,e

B
Y NOW THERE IS PROBABLY A GOOD BUZZ going in your workshop. Students are becoming more self-reliant, moving seamlessly around the room to find the supplies they need, and making decisions about what to add to their writing and when to begin a new piece. That self-reliance exists in part because you haven't pushed too hard for your children to write a lot. It's easy to be self-reliant when the task involves drawing stories, and harder when the work requires that a whole class of six-year-olds write up a storm. Today, then, you'll want to remember the instructions that are given to a cook: add flour slowly, stirring all the while. You'll teach—or remind—youngsters how to go about spelling hard words, and in doing so, you'll begin spotlighting the fact that writers don't just story-tell and draw. Writers also write. And writers write with the same resourcefulness and independence that you've been fostering all along.

Specifically, today's minilesson is Invented Spelling 101. This is a very basic minilesson, one that many kindergarten teachers have surely taught many times. It isn't meant to challenge your proficient spellers so much as to provide a baseline of essential knowledge that the whole class can draw upon—and that you can refer to during the small-group work you'll need to do with any children who find this difficult. In the minilesson, you will teach children to say a word, recording the sounds they hear at the start of the word, reread what they have written, and continue saying the rest of the word, listening to the very next sound, then again recording that sound, and so on. You'll help children refer to the alphabet chart when they aren't sure which letter or letters they should record for a particular sound. You'll emphasize listening for and recording *all* the sounds so that the words children write include beginning and ending, and now middle, sounds.

Today your goal will be to help all your children move toward meeting the rather low (in this dimension) Common Core State Standards that call for all first-graders to work toward segmenting single-syllable words into their complete sequence of individual sounds (phonemes), including digraphs and blends. This is a step up from kindergarten work when they learned to segment very simple CVC words and did their best to represent each sound with a letter. By the end of the year, first-graders will be expected to use conventional spelling for words with common spelling patterns (i.e., digraphs, short vowels, simple long vowel patterns) and frequently occurring irregular words (word wall words) and to spell more complex words phonetically, drawing on phonemic awareness and their knowledge of spelling conventions.

You may decide to use instructional resources and materials for word study such as the *Words Their Way* series by Donald Bear, Marcia Invernizzi, and Shane Templeton (2011) and also *Phonics Lessons* by Irene C. Fountas and Gay Su Pinnell (2003). If you are using a resource like these, you have probably begun analyzing your students' knowledge of words including their knowledge of word features (letters, spelling patterns) and the ways they use word-solving strategies when they write words. You might have administered a spelling inventory. By looking at an assessment like this and also studying your students' writing and spelling behaviors, you will see what they already know and also see their approximations to determine where to begin your word study instruction.

"It is important that what children learn in word study transfers to their work in writing workshop."

Using resources such as these, you are probably beginning your word study curriculum with an emphasis on short vowels, digraphs, and blends, in which case it will be important for students to attend to these features of words as they listen for each sound. You can help children begin to represent digraphs with two letters and to listen carefully for middle sounds in words and syllables. Middle sounds are often the most difficult sound for a child to isolate, and you should expect children to have some trouble discriminating between vowel sounds. While students are learning these features in word study, often practicing them through activities such as sorting and then making them with magnetic letters or letter tiles, it is important that

they are given support with transferring this knowledge to the context of writing. Some of this instruction can happen during word study through interactive writing and shared reading. It is also important that it happens during writing workshop. In this session you will demonstrate this work, problem-solving words as you write, demonstrating not only how you listen for each individual sound but also showing that you work a bit to figure out which letter or letters make a particular sound. It will help children if you show them that you sometimes use a tool to help, such as the alphabet chart or a class name chart.

Keep in mind that many children will come from kindergarten with a repertoire of sight words—words they "just know" and can write "in a snap"— such as *see*, *and*, *you*, and *like*. You can use assessments such as the TCRWP high-frequency word lists to see which words students know how to read with automaticity and then look to their writing to see which they also know how to spell correctly when writing. This information will help you decide which high-frequency words to study as a class and place on the word wall. At this point in the year, you may want to review some of the high-frequency words children learned in kindergarten, especially if they are ones your students are able to read but haven't completely mastered in their writing. Then you can begin adding a few words each week and remove words when most of the class can read and write them independently. You will want to show children how to use the word wall inside and outside of writing workshop.

Efficient spellers move between using their sight word knowledge and using their knowledge of letter sounds and spelling features such as blends and digraphs. Children need to learn to use both types of knowledge. You will probably find that some of your young writers have strong sight vocabularies, but you will want to notice if they try to write stories that contain only the words they already know how to spell. These youngsters need to be willing to take the risk of tackling an unfamiliar word.

The content of today's instruction, like the content of every day's instruction, needs to be combed through every day's writing workshop and through all of your one-to-one and small-group instruction.

Stretching Words to Spell Them

Hearing and Recording All Sounds

CONNECTION

Explain to students that writers say words they don't know slowly and write all the sounds so that people can read their writing.

"I've been watching you guys rereading your own stories—the ones you've put in your finished pocket. Sometimes it is hard to read your own writing, isn't it? Thumbs up if you've ever been rereading your own story and come to some letters that make no sense to you. You go, 'Huh? What does that say?' (See Figure 4–1.)

"It's a little frustrating, right? And pretty soon you will want to share your stories with other people, and the same thing will happen to them. They'll be reading along, so excited to know what happens next, and then, they won't be able to make out one of the words. They'll go, 'Huh? What does that say?'

By posing this question to the class, you invite children to be not just writers but also readers. It's important that children understand the reciprocal process of writing and reading. Meanwhile, you invite them also to self-assess, which is an essential component to growth.

I see a bumpy road.

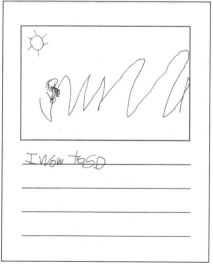

I was too scared.

I did it by myself.

FIG. 4–1   Ziekariba's story about riding his bike will be easier to read once he learns to hear and record more sounds in words and develops consistent spacing between words.

"When words are hard to read, the writer has usually got the first and the last sound—but sometimes the writer finds that the middle part of a word is hard. The thing is, if we want to reread our own stories and to let others read our stories too, we *need* to record *all* the sounds in those tricky words."

❖ **Name the teaching point.**

"Today I want to teach you that when you want to write a word you don't 'just know,' you've got to work hard to hear and write *all* the sounds. Say the word while you slide your finger slowly across the page, hear the first sound, and write that sound down. Read what you've written, sliding your finger under the letters. Hear the next sound, write it, and reread, sliding your finger. Do that until there are no more sounds."

This absolutely needs to be pantomimed so that students remember the steps of the strategy and so that you can use these gestures when prompting writers during conferences or small-group instruction.

TEACHING

Read what you have written so far and touch and tell the part of the story you want to write next.

"I started writing this story last night." (See Figure 4–2.)

> One snowy day I went sledding with my brother.

I turned the page. "On this next page, I already sketched my brother pushing me down the hill, but now I'm going to write, 'We went to the top of the hill and my brother gave me a big push. I went faster and faster down the hill.' I've already written 'We went to the top of the hill and my brother gave me a big.' Now I need to write the word *push*."

FIG. 4–2 Teacher's demonstration text in which she demonstrates and elicits help from her writers in problem-solving words. The sketches were already drawn, as she wanted to focus the students' attention on the work of writing the words.

Demonstrate the strategies you use to write words. Say the word you want to write slowly as you slide your finger across the space where you'll write. Listen for and record the first sound.

"Writers, help me write this word. Let's listen to the sound at the beginning of *push*. Let's say it very slowly while I slide my finger where the word will go. P-ush," we said repeatedly as I slid my finger across the space a few times, emphasizing listening for the beginning sound. "Do you hear a /p/ at the beginning of *push*? I do!" I wrote *p*.

Put your finger under the letter you've written and reread it. Say the rest of the word, sliding your finger, listening to the sounds that you haven't yet recorded. Repeat the process used above.

"Let's reread what we have written." I pointed under the *p* and read /p/. "Let me say the word slowly again and slide my finger as I try to hear the very next sound. P-u-sh. Let me hear that very next sound. I have to say it very slowly. P-u-sh. I hear /sh/. Wait! Is that the very *next* sound?" Again I said the word, this time concluding, "That's the last sound. Let's try again and see if there is a sound that we missed. P-uuuuu Oh! I hear /u/ like in *umbrella* on our alphabet chart." I pointed quickly to the alphabet chart. "It is the very next sound. I'll write that. Now I'll reread it and try to get that last sound. P-u-sh. /Sh/ /Sh/, like *she* or *shoe*. I know how to write that. It's an *s* and an *h*." I wrote it and then went back and reread, sliding my finger as I did, to check that I had recorded all the sounds.

Debrief by reminding children of the steps you've taken to hear and record all the sounds in a word.

"Writers, did you see that when I got to a word I didn't know how to spell, I did some hard work to figure out how to write it? I said the word slowly, slid my finger on the page where the word would go, listened carefully for the first sound, and then wrote it. I reread, saying the word and sliding my finger on the page until I heard the very next sound. Then I repeated until I heard and wrote all the sounds."

ACTIVE ENGAGEMENT

Help children spell the next tricky word, writing it on their white boards. Refer to the name chart for challenging letters or blends.

"I'm ready to write my next sentence: 'I went faster and faster down the hill.' I know the words *I* and *went*. Those are words I know in a snap, so I'll just write them quickly." I did.

"Let's reread this part of the story together so you can help me with the next word. 'I went . . .'"

The children chimed in, "Faster."

"Say *faster* and slide your finger where you will write it on your board. What's the first sound you hear?"

"/F/" many children called out.

The words you choose to problem solve in your demonstration should be chosen based on your students' stage of spelling development. This is different for each class. Look at your students' approximations in their writing to determine which words will be best for your lesson.

When you shift from the demonstration to debriefing, students should feel the different moves you are making just by the way your intonation and posture change. After most demonstrations, there will be a time for you to debrief, and that's a time when you are no longer acting like a writer. You are the teacher who has been watching the demonstration and now turns to talk, eye to eye with kids, asking if they noticed this or that during the previous portion of the minilesson.

"Great, write that!" I wrote an *f* in my booklet while students wrote on their boards. "Now put your finger under the first letter in the word, say the word slowly, and slide your finger. Listen for the very next sound."

The kids said the word and slid their fingers on their white boards, and I did this as well. They said, "faaaaaaaaster, faaaaaaa" and then voiced the next sound /a/! "It's an *a*!" many called. I signaled for them to write that.

"Let's reread and listen for the next sound. Fingers ready?" I asked as I put my finger under the first letter of the word. "Listen for the very next sound." Children again said the word several times, calling, "I hear /s/. It's /s/." Sabrina piped in, "I hear /st/ like *Stephen*."

"Great. The next two sounds go together to make /st/ like in Stephen's name. Let's look at our name chart to see how to spell /st/. Which two letters should we write? Stephen, can you help us out?" Stephen scrambled up and pointed to his name on the name chart. "Write those on your white board." Repeat the process with children until you've sounded out the rest of the word.

"Writers, here's the real trick. You all need to be able to do this work by yourselves, as you write your stories. Do you have the courage to try a hard word on your own?" The children called out that sure, they could try this. "Well, let me tell you what happened next, and you can choose your own hard word. After I got sledding faster and faster, there was a Boom! I smashed into a tree. Are any of you willing to try writing *boom*? How about *smashed*? Get your white board ready and go for it, all on your own. Remember, fingers ready as you say the word, listening for the first sound."

LINK

Remind children that the challenge is to spell on their own as they write their stories.

After a bit I said, "Even if you haven't finished, boards up. Hold them high so I can see what you have done so far!" The children held their white boards high. "Give yourselves a pat on the back. You did some really hard work today, hearing all the sounds in those tricky words. If you do that hard work today when you go to reread your story, you'll be able to read along easily. Remember that your readers, all the people who are waiting to hear your stories, need you to write down whole words, words with all their sounds marked. You'll need to do that for your whole life! And you can start doing that today, right now. Off you go!"

FIG. 4–3   A student's white board where he is problem solving the word *faster*

Supporting Writers as They Problem Solve Words

WHEN TEACHING FIRST-GRADE WRITERS, a good proportion of all your conferring and small-group work will be devoted to helping them become more proficient word solvers. As you approach individual writers, you will want to keep in mind where a particular child is in the stages of spelling development. This will help you decide what a child is ready to learn. As you study your writers, noticing patterns in spelling development and word-solving skills as well as in other aspects of their writing work, you'll group writers together who need the same type of support. A planning sheet (see Figure 4–4) can be helpful to use along with your conference note-taking sheet.

You will probably have a few children in your class who are emergent spellers. You'll spot these children quickly because even after today's lesson, they will use just a single letter to represent a word like Emani did in her story about going to the store, where she labeled parts of the picture using her knowledge of beginning sounds and then attempted to record words on the lines with some sounds in the words recorded accurately (see Figure 4–5).

> Page 1: I went to the store and we eat there. Labels: S-store; mom
> Page 2: I got a toy. Labels: S-store; M-me
> Page 3: I have a sister. She got a toy. Labels: S-store; Sa-sister

Alternatively, they may record whole sentences using strings of what seem like random letters or letter-like marks. These children need to develop a strong foundation in phonics. You'll want to work with them often during the writing workshop, as well as during word study time. Writing provides a perfect forum for helping these youngsters become secure in their letter-sound correspondence. Your goal will be for these children to know the sounds that letters make—starting with the consonants that make sounds that are heard in their names (e.g., the name *s* contains the sound /sssss/.) You'll teach children to use this knowledge to record the initial sounds in words, as well as the more dominant final sounds.

You will probably want these children to label lots of the objects in each of their pictures (perhaps instead of writing sentences or in addition to the sentences). These

Planning for Small-Group Instruction

Teaching Point:	Teaching Point:
Writers:	Writers:
Teaching Point:	Teaching Point:
Writers:	Writers:
Teaching Point:	Teaching Point:
Writers:	Writers:

FIG. 4–4   A small-group organizational tool that can be used during conferences to remind you of skills particular writers are ready to learn and that can be used to plan for strategy lessons. Often teachers jot the teaching point in the smaller box and then list the writers' names in the larger box.

writers will benefit from small-group work to help them stretch out a word and hear and isolate just the initial sound. You won't want to do the sounding out for these youngsters! They'll also benefit from using the alphabet chart. For example, a child who is trying to write *sun* can be taught to say the word and listen for the first sound. If the child doesn't know the letter that corresponds with that sound, she can look to the alphabet chart and find the picture that begins with the same sound. You might prompt the child by saying, "Say the word. Listen to what you hear at the beginning. Which picture on the alphabet chart has that same sound at the beginning? Great. Now let's look at the letter that makes that sound. Can you write that letter above the picture in your story?" Celebrate when these children label lots of pictures using initial sounds (even if they are not entirely correct). Move these children toward hearing final

"Writers, remember, too, that while some words require you to hear all the sounds, slowly and carefully, there are some words you just know (or are close to knowing), words you can spell in a snap. When you go to write a word, think, 'Is this one of those words I just know? Is this on the word wall?'

"Let's read over our word wall together to remind us of the words that are here." I used a pointer to touch the letter *A*, and then the words listed under it, with children reading chorally. We proceeded through the alphabet.

"If you were helping me write my sled story and I wanted to write that my face was so cold because I fell into the snow, what would I do to spell *was?* Tell the person beside you!

"Some of you said that I could just write it fast. I heard other children say I could look at the word wall. If I'm not sure exactly how to spell a word, but I know it is a word I'm learning how to write in a snap, then I can look at the word wall to find it. Right now, will all of you look at the word wall and point to *was* when you find

it?" As children scanned the word wall, I coached. "Some of you said the word to yourself and listened for the first sound, and you are looking for the different letters that make the /w/ sound to see if you can find *was*.

"Once you've found the word, look at it closely. Tell the person near you what you notice about how it is spelled. Now, without looking at the word wall, write *was* on your white boards. Go!" Children did this.

"Writers, you can use the word wall not only to help you spell a word, but you can also use it to help you check your spellings. Try that now. Reread whatever you have been writing today to someone near you, and when you get to a word that you think is on the word wall, stop. Then I want you and your listener to find the word on the word wall and study how it is spelled. Then look back at your writing to make sure your word looks right. If not, cross it out—the whole word—and look back at the word wall to help you write it."

As Students Continue Working . . .

"Can you hear that writers? I hear writers at the yellow table saying their words slowly again and again, really trying to make sure they get all the sounds down."

"Writers, remember, when you are done writing a word it is important to put a space after it. Use your finger if it helps you."

"Writers, Cooper just wrote the word *the* really fast. He wrote it in a snap!" (Snap your fingers.) "Remember that you all have words you 'just know,' words you don't have to sound out. When you get to one of those words, just picture it in your mind and write the letters as fast as you can!"

  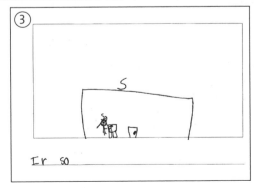

FIG. 4–5   Emani's story, about going to the store, shows her development of letter-sound correspondence and her use of this knowledge as she attempts to isolate and record initial sounds in words.

sounds as well. Many teachers provide these writers, if not all of their writers, with individual alphabet charts as well as with a class name chart. You might start out the year doing interactive writing with small groups of these children to get them doing some of this work with your support (see Figure 4–6).

You can write a story together and practice labeling the pictures and writing simple sentences, inviting students to do the work they are learning to do (beginning sounds, ending sounds) while you fill in the hard parts. Your temptation with these children will be to focus entirely on their spelling, and whereas this certainly merits consistent attention, you'll also want to help these youngsters tell coherent stories, even if they are labeling objects rather than writing sentences. Also know that these writers probably will work best on paper with only a couple lines because we want them to do most of their writing in the picture, whereas other writers will need three, four, or five lines on each page to encourage more sentences. It will be important to have a variety of paper choices and to talk to children about the paper that is best for them at this point in the year.

The majority of your class will be working toward hearing more than just the initial and ending sounds in words. You'll quickly identify the children who fall into this group because they'll be using most initial and final sounds and recording some middle sounds, often incorrectly. Today's minilesson is perfectly aimed to support these writers, but they'll need small-group work or one-to-one coaching to begin doing this independently. If you find that some of these children don't hear the middle sound unless you overemphasize it while sounding a word out for them, then be sure that instead of becoming the sounder-outer for these children, you give them more practice hearing and isolating the middle sound in words. You can coach these children to separate the sounds in simple CVC words. *Cat* is /c/ /a/ /t/. If many children need this support, which is likely, you might sing a warm-up song (to the tune of "London Bridge Is Falling Down"): Listen to the word I say, word I say, word I say. / Tell me all the sounds you hear. / Listen to this word: *pin*.

Students then segment the word, isolating every sound and saying each in sequence. You might set children up so they each have three sound boxes (for CVC words, such as *cat*) in front of them, and you might channel students to say the word slowly, touching each box as they say each sound. Keep in mind that the challenge here is helping

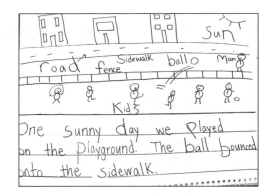

FIG. 4–6   Interactive writing

the *children* both say and hear all the individual sounds. You will want to refrain from doing the work for them!

You will also have students who are already recording beginning, middle, and ending sounds. These writers are ready to be hearing parts of words, including short vowel word families (*-an, -at, -op, -un*) that will soon be taught during word study, blends (*sl* in *slide*), and digraphs (*sh* in *shop*) and making connections to known words rather than writing sound by sound. This work will allow them to be more efficient solvers of words, and they will be able to get more words down in a writing session. There will be an entire session in Bend II devoted to the work of using known words to write new words and hearing and recording parts of words. Session 12 can help you coach these youngsters.

Notice not only children's abilities to spell words they don't know, but also their knowledge of sight vocabulary. Chances are good that many of your children know at least twenty words "by heart," and they may not use what they know as they write. These writers will need support with recognizing when a word is one that they "just know." (Some teachers call them "snap words," because the kids know them in a snap.) Children should learn to recognize when they know a word, to make a mental picture of that word, and to write it as fast as they can without sounding it out. Today's mid-workshop teaching will provide the whole class with support with snap words, and in some classes, an entire session may be needed around using these words.

Ways to Spell Words

Ask children to turn and talk about strategies they use to write tricky words. Listen in and harvest a few more strategies for word solving.

"Writers, you have been using so many powerful ways to write tricky words that I started a chart of what I noticed." I pointed to the "Ways to Spell Words" chart, with the first bullet prewritten. "I saw many of you stretching out the words today, saying them slowly, sliding your finger, and listening for all the sounds in the word." I pointed to the chart. "That is one way to spell words that are new to you. I know some of you were spelling words other ways, like using the word wall when you were checking your writing. But I bet you have even *more* ways to spell words. Look back at your writing right now and find a tricky word that you spelled all by yourself. Show that word to a person near you and tell that person how you went about spelling the word."

As the children talked, I listened in and heard comments such as, "I spelled *and* because I looked at the word wall and found it under the *a*."

"I knew it from kindergarten. It's a snap word. I can spell it fast—s-e-e see!"

"I knew how to write *fall* because it has *all* in it. I just know how to spell *all*—it's easy."

Reconvening the class, I said, "Writers, I heard some of you say that there are some words you just knew how to write—words you could write in a snap. You didn't need to slow down to spell those words. I'll add 'use snap words' to the chart. I also heard some of you saying that some words have little words inside them—like inside *fall* is *all*. That's a great strategy. I'll add that to the chart. When we get to a word, we have to think, 'What strategy works best for me?'" (See Figure 4–7.)

FIG. 4–7 "Ways to Spell Words" chart

Ways to Spell Words

- Say it, slide it, hear it, write it
- Use snap words
- Listen for little words inside

Zooming In
Focusing on Small Moments

IN THIS SESSION, you'll teach children that writers write with focus.

GETTING READY

✔ Construction paper watermelon with Velcro dots as seeds, so that they can be easily removed when showing how you can pick just one seed to write a story (or other visual) (see Connection)

✔ Mentor text, *Night of the Veggie Monster*

✔ Your own Small Moment story (see Teaching)

✔ A blank booklet to use in the teaching part of the lesson

✔ Published books you have read to your class and that your children are familiar with that exemplify small moments with details (e.g., *The Relatives Came* [Rylant 1993], *The Kissing Hand* [Penn 2007], *Shortcut* [Crews 1996], *A Chair for My Mother* [Williams 1982]) (see Share)

Y OU'LL SEE that often in our units of study for the primary grades, you will run from one side of the boat to another, teaching first an emphasis on phonics and spelling and then an emphasis on content and craft. Both matter, and to young writers, very little is automatic yet.

From yesterday's focus on spelling, this session shifts to an examination of craft and specifically invites children to focus their narratives so that the stories they write live up to the name Small Moment stories. There are many reasons why I emphasize focus, but a word of caution: This unit has been piloted in tens of thousands of classrooms, and the results have been remarkable, with many teachers and parents saying in amazement, "I had absolutely no idea my kids could write like that!" However, many teachers interpreted our emphasis on writing focused narratives as the letter of the law and have insisted that every story every child write be absolutely focused. An account of looking for and finding a lost dog becomes a zoomed-in account of the moment when Mom returns home with the dog.

But your children are still just learning about how stories go, and although their writing will be far more charming and probably more effective when they focus in on a tighter narrative, the truth is that it is just fine for a child to write on page 1 about the lost dog, on page 2 about the search, and on page 3 about the reunion. It would even be fine if the story ended with a party celebrating the dog's return! Also, keep in mind that focus and detail are important—but not more important than writers writing a lot, with fluency and voice.

Having backed away a bit from what has sometimes turned out to be an overemphasis on the importance of focus, I do want to say that if the goal is to improve children's writing, I know of no easier way to accomplish this than to teach youngsters how to focus in on smaller moments, writing the story of single events. By limiting the size—the scope—of a subject, details emerge that make all the difference. In this session, you will teach your students to write about one small time instead of writing "about everything" stories.

Zooming In
Focusing on Small Moments

CONNECTION

Name the work that children have been doing that calls for them to learn a new strategy.

"Writers, when you think about true stories that you could write, some of you are coming up with great big giant topics like, 'I could write about my life' or 'I could write about school.'" I gestured to show these topics are so huge that I staggered under the weight of them. "You may have heard this in kindergarten, but sometimes we call those 'watermelon topics' because they are so big. They are so big, in fact, that just like they are hard to carry, they are hard to write! Jessica has been writing and writing and she has only gotten to the very beginning of what she wants to say because she is trying to write everything. She's trying to write the whole watermelon! Stop and think for a moment. Does your story feel like you are carrying a watermelon? Does it feel like you will have to write and write and write and that you have to tell *everything*? Thumbs up if you know what I mean."

❖ **Name the teaching point.**

"Today I want to teach you that instead of writing about big (watermelon) topics, writers write about teeny tiny (seed) stories—little stories inside the one big topic. And the cool thing is that inside a watermelon topic there are a zillion teeny tiny seed stories!"

TEACHING

Tell children that the mentor author probably first thought of a big, general watermelon topic and then decided to focus on a tiny seed story.

"I'm pretty sure that when George McClements sat down to write (like we'll do soon) he probably had a few big, huge topics on his mind. I think of them as watermelon topics." I used my hands to illustrate the size of a watermelon story. "He probably thought, 'I *could* write about my vacation,'" my hands showed this would be a watermelon topic, "or about eating food with my family." Again, my hands showed this would be another watermelon topic.

"But here is the thing. George knows that great story writers don't usually write about big huge watermelon topics. Instead, great story writers know that inside any one of those topics there are a zillion little seed stories. Like inside the

You might want to use yourself as an example in this connection. You could describe how you realized your writing is going for a whole page and you haven't even hinted at the important part yet!

You will want to decide how the author you have selected can help children with beginning their writing process. You won't want to say "George Clements wrote about his son putting on veggie monster performances and you can write about veggies too," because you are hoping children learn strategies (not topics) from authors they admire.

topic 'eating with my family' George could have written about taking his son to the pancake house or about how he makes these fantastic meatballs and his son can eat five at a time, or about when his son learned to eat with chopsticks. His writing would have gone on and on and on, with just one sentence about each of those things: we went to the pancake house *and* my son learned to eat with chopsticks *and* he ate the fantastic meatballs I made *and.* . . .

"But George decided not to write all about a watermelon topic—like all about eating with his family—and instead he chose just one tiny seed, one tiny story. So he wrote just about *one* time when his son, who can't stand vegetables, put his parents through one of his 'veggie monster performances' while facing a plate of peas."

Use a shared class experience to demonstrate picking just one small story from a big watermelon topic.

"When you write, you'll want to take lessons from what George has done, and to ask yourself, 'Wait. Is this a watermelon topic?' Let's say you decided to write about today in school. Think to yourself, 'Is that a teeny tiny seed story,'" and I gestured to show picking up a watermelon seed, "'or a giant watermelon topic?'" Again I gestured. The children gestured that it would be a watermelon topic.

"If I wrote a story about a big huge topic like that, my story wouldn't have any details. It might go, 'We had morning meeting,'" I touched one seed in a sketch of a watermelon slice, "*and* we went to art class." I touched another. "*And* our rabbit, Magic, jumped out of the crate." I touched another seed. "*And* Josh's dad came to talk to us about recycling." I touched another seed. "Wow! That is a *gigantic* watermelon story with a lot of seed stories.

"But we can learn from George that good story writers pick a teeny tiny seed story. I think I'm going to write about just one of those seeds that was in my big topic! I'll write about Magic jumping out of the crate." I picked up a booklet, and touched the first page. "Hmm, how did *that* story begin? Shall I start with all of us walking back from art?" I shook my head. "That is from another seed. Not the one story about Magic. Art class doesn't fit with our Bunny Escape story. Shall I begin right before we noticed that he had escaped from his cage? Let's think for a moment about how a seed story could start." I paused to let everyone think. "It could go like this."

> I heard a strange shuffling noise. I looked over at Magic's cage and the door was open and Magic was jumping off the counter!

I turned the page.

Debrief, reminding children to pick just one small story (seed), from a big topic (watermelon) they might be inclined to tell.

"Writers, did you see how I had this big watermelon topic filled with all the stories of what we did today, but then I picked just one seed, one small story? And now we would tell, sketch, and write it across the pages. You can do this, too."

This metaphor has been helpful in lots of K–1 classrooms, but a few children interpret the term watermelon topic *literally and write about watermelons and seeds! Be mindful that metaphors can be confusing to children who are English language learners. Don't bypass metaphor, but do explicitly tell them what you mean. "You know how watermelons are big? Well, when I say 'watermelon topic' I mean a big topic such as. . . ."*

Remember you can use your mentor text to support different aspects of writing. Often teachers use the mentor text to highlight small craft moves. Keep in mind that a mentor text can be used as an example of other aspects of writing, including structure.

ACTIVE ENGAGEMENT

Ask the children to try to think of another seed story, using the same shared watermelon topic that you used in your demonstration.

"Right now, think back to our big watermelon topic of what happened so far today, but this time, *you* pick just one seed story that you want to tell. Take a minute and when you get the seed story in your head, give me a thumbs up."

Channel children to rehearse for this story by touching and telling across the pages of an imaginary booklet.

"Think about how your story went. What happened first? Make sure the first thing that happened really fits with the story instead of being a part of another seed. Then think about what happened next and at the end. Now pretend you have a booklet with three pages in your hand. Say the words you will write on each page aloud to the person next to you."

After listening in for a few moments, I redirected the students to stop and look at me while I shared what I noticed. "I heard Ronald say he was going to write *just* about the time in art class when he splattered paint all over his shirt! And I heard Rachel say, 'I am *not* going to write about everything. I am *only* going to write about Josh's dad showing us those recycled plastic bottles.'"

Give students repeated practice at identifying seed stories inside big watermelon topics.

"Let's practice finding other seed stories inside big watermelon topics. Here is a big watermelon topic: playing with a friend. Thumbs up if you have one friend in mind and you are thinking of the things you have done when you play together. Now, is playing with a friend a watermelon topic or a seed story?" The children agreed it was a watermelon topic. "Think of one particular thing you did when you played with your friend, one fun—or bad—time you had. Thumbs up if you thought of that!" The children put their thumbs up.

"Okay, you've got that one. Here's another. Is this a watermelon topic or a seed story? Things you like to do in winter." I paused to give them time to think. The children agreed it was a watermelon topic, and with coaching, they selected one particular thing they did one winter as a potential seed story.

LINK

Remind writers that when they write narratives, it always helps to pause and ask, "Is this a watermelon topic?" in which case it is important to focus it more.

"Writers, today and every day when you go to write a story, remember to pause and to ask, 'Is this a watermelon topic or a seed story?' If you have a great big watermelon topic, you can ask, 'What is one specific thing I did that could make a good story?' You'll find there are a zillion seed stories inside each watermelon topic."

Supporting Students as They Write More Focused Narratives

TODAY IS AN EXCITING DAY for you and the students because it is the day you will begin to see your students' stories take more of the shape you've been hoping for. Today they may realize that they have so many more stories to tell—the stories they have inside their watermelon topics. While many of your students will *begin* to focus their writing on one time they did something, you will have writers who will need support with this—writers who write about everything they did in a day or on a trip and who continued to do this during today's active engagement. If you plan to help these writers today, the following transcript might be helpful. In it, you'll see how I tend to help students who need support writing more focus.

Shariff flipped through his multiple-page story, beginning to sketch on his last page. "What are you working on as a writer today, Shariff?" I asked as I knelt down next to him. As a response, Shariff turned to the first page and began reading his writing aloud.

"This is me playing baseball. I am getting strawberry ice cream. I am climbing the stairs. I am getting into bed. I am reading a story."

"Wow. What a busy evening! Shariff, you seem to be the kind of writer who really loves to share a lot about your life, and you include details. For example, here where you told me the kind of ice cream you had. And then how you told me that you climbed the stairs because you were going to bed. That really helps the reader picture what happened!" I was naming for Shariff what he was doing as a writer to help him develop a writing identity, to help him get to know the kind of writer he is. I can build on this once I begin teaching. Shariff smiled as he looked back at his story.

I knew I wanted to teach Shariff to focus on one event at a time. I decided to begin the teaching by helping Shariff discover that he had written multiple stories in his booklet. "So, Shariff, I have a question about your story. Did you take that ice cream with you into bed?" He laughed and shook his head. "Oh, so the ice cream and going to bed don't fit together in the same story. Are they two different stories?" He looked at me

MID-WORKSHOP TEACHING
Writers Stay in the Moment—Even at the End

"Writers, eyes up here for one minute please. Wow! Look at the small, seed stories you have been writing! Before you finish your stories, I want to tell you a very special trick for ending small moment stories. If you end your story with 'and then I went home,' or 'and then I went to sleep,'" I said in a fast, flat tone, "there is a problem. Both endings are not part of your moment, are not part of *this* seed. So many of your stories start in the moment with that first thing that happened. Your ending needs to do that too. It is important for the ending to stay in the moment so your reader doesn't get confused and think you are starting to tell a new story. Here is the trick. To write a good ending that connects to what your story is about, writers can think, 'What is the *very* next thing that happened?' and write that, especially if it is sort of an ending thing." (See Figure 5–1.)

"For example, Heather was just about to write the ending to her story about her brother's graduation. She thought to herself, 'Now, what happened next?' She reread the part about more and more people coming and thought, 'Well, after that, we went home.' But then she said, 'Wait, no. That didn't happen right after.' Then, she thought, 'What is the *very* next thing that happened?' And she said, 'Oh, yeah! My brother gave me a hug and I said congratulations. Let me write that.' Writers, did you see how Heather ended her Small Moment story about her brother's graduation by writing the *very* next thing that happened, not about stuff that happened much later? If your writing needs an ending soon, you might try this out. Add this strategy to all the things you can try as you write!"

FIG. 5–1 Heather's story about her brother's graduation in which she ends in the moment

curiously, telling me that he hadn't thought about this possibility. "Shariff, remember today how I was thinking about how I could write about something that happened at school and I thought about how I could write about so many things that happened? Each page would have been a different thing, like a giant watermelon story filled with smaller stories like seeds. It would be hard to give this book a title because you've got the baseball story, the ice cream cone story, the going to bed story! All of these are great ideas, and I want to teach you today how writers choose just one story to stretch out. Instead of jamming a whole lot of stories into one book, writers choose one seed story and focus on that. So what will you choose? The baseball game? The ice cream cone?"

"The ice cream one was funny. I loved making the strawberry ice cream cone. It was a big cone with two scoops! It was dripping down my arm." Reaching into the air, Shariff said, "The cone was like *this* big!"

Duly impressed both with the ice cream cone and with his ability to retell the incident, I said, "I have never heard of a cone that big. Wow! And I can picture it dripping down your arm. How could you even begin to eat it fast enough, right? You could write another book about just the ice cream part! I'll show you."

I took hold of a new booklet. Turning the pages, I said, "You can get another booklet like this, and on all these pages, you can stretch out just that small moment of getting the big ice cream cone. You can tell about the two scoops, and you can tell us how it dripped down your arm."

Shariff was thrilled. "Yes, I want to do that!"

"Let's plan it out first. Will it start with you telling your mom you wanted two scoops? Or with you coming into the kitchen for ice cream? Or what?"

"I want to start with the two scoops!"

At this point I wanted to name what Shariff had done as a writer and remind him to do this often in future writing. "Shariff, instead of telling about everything you did—the baseball game, the ice cream cone, the going upstairs, the big watermelon topic—you picked just one seed, one tiny story from that big watermelon topic, and now you're planning to stretch it across three pages, writing about just that moment! Writers do that! And you can do that whenever you write."

You can do this same work in a strategy lesson with a slightly different strategy. You can convene a group of writers who have separate stories on each page or who have a page that doesn't fit. You can ask the writers to reread their stories and decide what one thing their story is about and to give the book a title. Then have them reread and ask, "Does this page fit with my title?" If it does, the page stays. If it doesn't, you could teach the writers to take the page out and use it to write another story. You will need to have the paper and the stapler close by so you can give students blank pages to add to their stories. By physically rearranging pages, you are giving children a concrete experience with revising. If students seem hesitant, you may need to demonstrate with a piece of your own first, because this will give them the confidence to do the same work of tearing off pages with their own stories.

Once they have their new booklets ready to go, you may need to coach them to think about where the story starts, because it is important that they learn to begin and end their stories in ways that connect to the important part. Once they've done that, they can sketch and write, so you could send them off to continue working, reminding them that as they plan future stories, they will want to think about that one thing, that one seed idea, from inside their watermelon topics.

Looking to Mentor Texts to Add Detail to Our Writing

Set the stage for cherishing details in stories. Read aloud excerpts from a few published stories that are filled with details, sharing with children the parts you love and letting them have a chance to find parts they love.

"Writers, have you ever been someplace—like at the beach or walking down a city sidewalk—and suddenly, you spot some tiny little thing that is so cool that it stops you in your tracks and you get down on your knees to see it, and you call to others, 'Hey, look, there is this really cool thing you almost walked right past!'? I've always felt that little kids are the best at spotting those tiny little details that others would just walk right past—like a buttercup flower growing in the crack between two squares of the sidewalk or a tiny little fossil imprinted into a beach stone.

"Here's the thing. There are tiny jewels like one precious buttercup in good stories, too. Some people read right past them. But kids and authors, both, notice those tiny little gems and say to everyone else, 'Wait, slow down. Did you see this?!'

"I'm going to read you just a bit of a famous story by a writer like you who writes about small moments from her life. It's Cynthia Rylant's *The Relatives Came*. You've heard it before, so it should sound familiar. Here's a tiny little detail that other people might miss if they weren't paying attention. It's part of a description of the relatives gathering in her house and going to sleep. Remember when they all went to sleep without an extra bed?"

> *So a few squeezed in with us and the rest slept on the floor, some with their arms thrown over the closest person, or some with an arm across one person and a leg across another. It was different, going to sleep with all that new breathing in the house.*

"Did you notice how Cynthia talked about all those people in the house by telling about 'all that new breathing' and by telling us about the ten hugs that take place just between the kitchen and the living room? Can't you just see that house packed full of aunts and uncles and cousins?

"Now listen to the tiny details in *The Kissing Hand*, of how Chester kisses his mother's hand."

> *Chester took his mother's hand in his own and unfolded her large, familiar fingers into a fan. Next, he leaned forward and kissed the center of her hand. "Now you have a Kissing Hand, too," he told her.*

"Isn't it fun to share parts of writing that we love? Writers, turn and tell the person sitting next to you the details you liked in that description, and tell each other what these details make you want to try or add in your own writing."

Here, we choose Cynthia Rylant's The Relatives Came *and Audrey Penn's* The Kissing Hand *because our children are familiar with these stories from our daily read-alouds. You will of course want to choose stories that are familiar to your children, ones they've heard before, so the focus is on the strategy at hand and not the content of the story.*

Partnerships and Storytelling

You HAVE GIVEN CHILDREN TIME each day to write independently, tools they need, models of what others have written, and explicit instruction. All this is necessary—but not sufficient. Writers also need company. You will have given children chances to talk during "turn-and-talk" interludes in previous minilessons, allowing children to turn to the person next to them and share an observation or practice a strategy. These tiny conversations are more efficient and valuable if the child returns to the same partner each day—at least for a stretch of weeks. In today's lesson, then, you establish long-term partnerships.

It will be important to think through the partnerships you establish. Although you are still getting to know your students, by now you have some sense of their personalities and strengths, which is good because this can help you develop partnerships that last for at least a few months. I highly recommend keeping the partnerships you create now together for the entire unit, preferably for the year. If you feel like a partnership is not working or that the whole class would benefit from a change mid-year, that would be a good time to switch partnerships. Successful pairing of students in your classroom not only will nurture children's writing, but will nurture their friendships, too. You will also need to organize meeting places for partners to work together throughout the workshop. Most teachers find it helps for partners to sit next to each other in both the meeting area and during work time. How will you announce the partnerships you establish? Will you set folders out on tables before the workshop begins, with writers sitting beside each other, and with one partner named Partner 1 and the other Partner 2? One of the challenges will be to handle the logistics of partnerships with enough grace that they do not overwhelm everything else, deflating the excitement of this occasion.

Of course, once partnerships are established, children need to know the different jobs partners do together. Your students will come from kindergarten knowing that writing partners tell each other their ideas for writing and rehearse their stories together before writing them. Hopefully they know how to take turns listening and speaking, and this work today will continue to support them with this basic, yet important, skill as described in

IN THIS SESSION, you'll teach children that writers talk to other writers about their writing, storytelling their ideas out loud.

GETTING READY

✔ Each child's name on a piece of paper, organized on the rug so that partners' names are next to each other. For each partnership, put a number 1 on one partner's paper and a number 2 on the other partner's paper. (see Connection)

✔ A child who will act as your writing partner in the minilesson and a story in mind to rehearse with this child (see Teaching)

✔ Blank booklet for demonstrating how to tell a story with a partner (see Teaching)

✔ "Storytelling with a Partner" chart, with the four steps prewritten (see Teaching)

✔ "How to Write a Story" chart (see Active Engagement)

COMMON CORE STATE STANDARDS: W.1.3, W.1.5; RL.1.1; SL.1.1, SL.1.2, SL.1.3, SL.1.4; L.1.1, L.1.2

the Speaking and Listening Common Core Standards for first-graders. Despite the foundation laid for them in kindergarten, though, they may or may not be accustomed to giving each other feedback yet, especially feedback that leads to revision.

"This minilesson can help you get started lifting the level of partnership interactions by showing writers that they have jobs to do in their partnerships throughout all parts of the writing process."

Today, then, you'll lay the groundwork for the concept that partners offer each other concrete and specific suggestions, and these suggestions help their partners revise. In the CCSS, it states that we should aim for our first-graders, by the end of the year, to be able to "with guidance and support from adults, focus on a topic, respond to questions and suggestions from peers, and add details to strengthen writing as needed" (W.1.5). Establishing these partnerships will support this peer collaboration. But even more than that, this minilesson can help you get started lifting the level of partnership interactions by showing writers that they have jobs to do in their partnerships throughout all parts of the writing process.

For today, you will teach partners that before writing time begins they can help each other plan their stories—storytelling stories not just once, but twice, nudging them to retell the story more clearly. The mid-workshop teaching and the share can show writers other jobs partners have later in the writing process.

Partnerships and Storytelling

CONNECTION

Tell children that they have met *most* of the conditions writers need to write.

"Writers, as you come to the meeting area today, I need each of you to find the paper that has your name on it and to sit where your name is." Once the children had settled into their new spots, I began.

"Writers, we've talked a lot about what writers need to do their best work. We know writers need tools," I held up a pen, pencil, and folder to illustrate, "and you have your toolboxes." I held up a box with the supplies I had introduced. "We know writers need paper, too, so you have your booklets." I held up paper. "But writers need one more thing.

"Sometimes, to get their thinking going, writers talk with other writers. They need company. And often, they get together with one person who becomes their special writing friend—their writing partner—and plan what they will write."

Prior to this minilesson, you need to mentally divide the class into partnerships. Consider ability levels, friendships, and behavior issues. These partnerships will probably be mixed-ability partnerships (although certainly don't set one partner up as the teacher for the other). If you need to have a triad, be careful because this can be a difficult social arrangement.

Tell children that today they'll plan with a writing partner.

"You'll see your name and your partner's name on a piece of paper. You'll see that the papers say that one of you is Partner 1 and one is Partner 2. Every day, for every minilesson and every share from now on, you and your partner will sit at the place where your names are now, beside each other. And I've changed your seats during writing time so you'll sit near your writing partner during writing time too. Later when you go off to write, you can find your new writing seats."

❖ **Name the teaching point.**

"Today I want to teach you that writers have partners who help them with their writing. One way writing partners help each other is by helping each other plan how their stories will go. They tell each other their stories, using the exact words they will write, and then try to tell the stories *again* with even more details."

This is just one possible way to manage the chaos this minilesson threatens to create. Often teachers will find other solutions. The real point is that we need to predict when our teaching ideas will have management ramifications, and to find ways to maintain efficiency and order.

TEACHING

With one child serving as your partner, touch the pages of your book and tell your story to your partner, who then asks questions to help her understand more of the story. After elaborating, again "touch and tell" the now-expanded story.

"Let me show you how I meet with my writing partner. Watch closely, because this is what you are going to be doing from now on.

"Ariel will be my partner. First, we decide whether Partner 1 or Partner 2 will plan. We decided I am the one planning first today, so I will tell my story now, and my partner will listen. I am going to think of the story I want to write and then tell it to my partner as I touch the pages of my booklet. I'm going to think first. You think with me about your story and how it will go." I paused and struck a thinking pose.

"Here is my story." I touched each blank page as I said the words I would soon write on the page:

> One day I made a birthday cake for a neighbor. I put the icing on.

I turned the page.

> I opened the can of sprinkles.

I turned the page.

> The sprinkles went all over the cake and everywhere.

I turned to Ariel and asked her if she had any questions about my story. She hesitated, then said, "So did the sprinkles get messed up?"

I responded, "Yes, they went all over the floor and on me too."

Ariel then asked, "How come the sprinkles went on the floor? Why didn't you put them on the cake?"

I said, "I wanted to put them on the cake but when I pulled the lid off, it popped and then all the sprinkles came out by mistake."

Ariel laughed, and said, "You should tell that! It is a funny story." I agreed that I should write the story with all the new stuff in it, and with my partner's urging, first touched the pages and said aloud the new story.

> One day I made a birthday cake for my neighbor. I put the icing on the cake.

Partnerships are especially important if some of your students are English language learners because these children need language input more than anything. Try to partner children so that no two who speak Mandarin are partners. If you aren't certain which child speaks which language, you need to find out. Ask the class for help. You'll also find it helpful to partner children so that one has stronger English skills than the other. Under no circumstances can you allow an English language learner to be isolated because "he doesn't speak English." The child needs just the opposite!

I turned the page.

I tried to open the sprinkles can to put them on cake, but the top popped off.

I turned the page.

The sprinkles went all over the floor and on me. But some went on the cake, too!

Debrief in ways that help children extrapolate the sequence they can use when rehearsing with a partner.

"Ariel, you helped me so much! Writers, I hope you all can have a partner who helps you—or that you can *be* that helping partner. Remember, one partner tells the story he or she plans to write. The other partner listens and tries to picture the whole story. Usually the partner needs to ask some questions or wants to hear more. After that," and I pointed to step 3 on the chart, "the storytelling partner, Partner 1, tells the story *again*, putting in more information— more details."

Storytelling with a Partner

1. First partner tells the story.

2. Next partner pictures it and asks questions.

3. First partner tells the story <u>again</u>, saying more!

4. Partners switch!

ACTIVE ENGAGEMENT

Channel Partner 1s to get ready to touch and tell their story, getting Partner 2s ready to listen with intensity, aiming to envision or enact the story.

"Right now, Partner 1, please do what I just did, and Partner 2, will you try to be as helpful to your partner as Ariel was to me? Partner 2s, give me a thumbs up." They signaled. "Will you look like this when you are listening?" I picked at my teeth and looked to the opposite side of the room, turning my back on the class.

The children all chorused, "No!"

"Let me see intense listening." I pointed to step 1, and said, "Partner 1, ready? Go!"

Some charts such as the "How to Write a Story" chart will stay up for the entire unit and often will live on the classroom wall all year except for changes that are made to support a particular type of writing as the units change. Other charts such as this storytelling one will be brought out at certain times during the unit, such as during a partner time, or will remain up until most of the writers have internalized the steps or strategies.

As half the class told their story to another child, I moved quickly among the children, reminding one to say aloud the actual words she planned to write—not to talk *about* the eventual story but instead to dictate it. I reminded another to listen in such a way that he could picture, and almost reenact, the story he was hearing, asking questions that emerged from that intense listening. I helped another child know that when in doubt, who, where, when, and why questions often work, referring back to the questions on the "How to Write a Story" chart.

After a moment, I intervened. "Writers, you have added so much information in response to your partner's questions. But here is the trick. Can you now go back to the start of the story and tell it with a lot more detail and feeling because you know what your listener needs to know and because you are writing for a listener? Partner 1, touch and tell again, and this time make what you say is so, so much richer than your first time."

LINK

Set children up to use all that they have learned as they begin to write.

"Let's reread the partner chart to remind us of how you and your partner can take turns anytime you are planning how your stories will go." I proceeded to read the chart aloud as the children chimed in. "Partner 2, I know you haven't had time to share yet. For now, touch and tell your story and ask *yourself* questions, so that you write a ton all on your own.

"Today when you go back to your seats, both of you can start writing right away. And I hope you'll remember all the things you've learned so far. Remember, you are the writer, so you know what your writing needs. *You* need to remember all you have learned and figure out which strategies and which ideas to use today to help you. If you are going to remember what you've learned and figure out what to do in your writing today, stand up and take a bow. I can't wait to watch *all* the things you all do as you get started on your writing. Off you go."

Channel Partners and Small Groups to Increase Support

TODAY SOME OF YOUR CONFERRING AND SMALL-GROUP TIME will be spent with writing partners, especially those who need support in planning stories and those who need support with writing in clear, easy-to-read ways.

◆ Writers who continue to need support with telling a cohesive story with a beginning, middle, and end or need support in including important details such as who, what, and where will benefit from having a partnership conference around storytelling. These may be writers who during the minilesson could be heard describing the topics they planned to write about rather than saying the actual words they intended to write. You can coach partners to remind each other to story-tell on their fingers, using storytelling words such as "One day . . . After that . . . Then . . . " and provide them with a small chart with picture cues and question words (Who? Where? What? When? How?) to help remind them of questions they can ask their partners as well as what to include in their story as they tell it.

◆ You are probably finding that there are writers who are having difficulty rereading their writing because there may be words with few letters or missing words. You can invite the writing partner into the conference and show the partners how to reread each other's writing together, putting the writing between them, pointing together under each word, and helping each other work through the tricky parts. You can teach the partner to prompt the writer to reread on his or her own, saying things such as, "Look at the picture. What would make sense?" or "That doesn't look right. Let's fix it." This way the partners are prepared to do the coaching you can't always provide. Session 7 will teach writers how to do this for themselves as they write, but some writers really need the support of their partner to get into this habit of checking their writing.

Some of your time with students will also be used to support them with skills from previous sessions. Look back at the five lessons you taught and reread the conferring write-ups to think about teaching priorities for groups of students.

◆ Some students may need continued support with coming up with ideas and rehearsing those stories. You can bring those writers together and have them practice thinking of an idea and telling it across their fingers.

(continues)

MID-WORKSHOP TEACHING
Partners Also Help *During* Writing Time

"Writers, partners don't just help writers *before* they write. They also help writers *during* writing time. If you don't know what else to write, you can ask your writing partner to help you. Are you ready to hear one more thing partners can do?"

Children nodded. "Here it is: you can ask your partner to look at your *pictures* and ask you question that get you to say more. Ariel and I did this too. Ariel looked at my picture and saw there were four children in it. Ariel said, 'I didn't know about other people. Who else was there?'

"I answered, 'Wow, I forgot to add those important details. All my neighbors were there and we were working on this together. I better add that! What else do you see in the pictures that I forgot to say in the words?'

"And she told me more. My partner helped me by looking at the pictures. So now I have a lot to add!

"Writers, when you are stuck during writing time, you can ask your partner for help, and your partner can listen to your story, look at your illustrations, and ask questions. To practice, right now, Partner 1, will you help Partner 2?"

◆ Other writers will benefit from support with moving from sketches to getting sentences down on the page. Help them touch parts of the sketch and tell the story of the page before writing the words. They may need to practice storytelling one page multiple times until they know how it goes and can remember the words.

◆ Students who continue to move from one story to the next without revising, especially students who are already writing a sentence on each page, will benefit from continued coaching to go back and add more. Once writers are writing one sentence on a page, they can write two!

◆ Yesterday's lesson provided explicit instruction around spelling, and you probably now have a better picture of how writers in your class problem solve words. It is especially important to support two groups in particular with spelling work. One group is writers who get stuck easily and want help writing words, waiting for you or someone at their table to help them. They need to practice using what they know and the tools they have (e.g., the alphabet chart) to spell independently. The other group is the group of students who do know a lot about words. They know their letters and sounds and can read some sight words but aren't showing that in their writing. It is important to show students how to transfer what they know about words to their own writing. Small-group interactive writing can help with this.

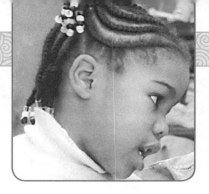

Rereading and Anticipating a Partner's Questions

Tell children that writers add to their writing by imagining the questions their partners might ask.

After convening the class in the meeting area with their stories and pencils, I said, "Writers, you see how partners help you make your writing better? Partners can help you plan your stories, they can look at and listen to your stories, and ask you questions so that you can elaborate your ideas. But guess what? Your partner can help you even when you are working by yourself. Whenever you sit down to write, *imagine* that your partner is right there with you, looking over your shoulder, reading your book. Think, 'What would my partner want to know? What questions would she ask?' Then try to answer those questions by adding to your writing.

"Let's give this a try right now. Go to the page you are writing. Reread what you've written and think, 'What would my partner want to know?' Remember, don't read to your partner. Read your work to yourself and *pretend* your partner is listening.

"Thumbs up when you have a question you think your partner would ask." When most of the writers had put their thumbs up, I asked a couple of students to share. Jesse said, "I think my partner would say, 'Who did you go to soccer practice with?'"

Then Myles said, "My partner would say, 'Where did you play Legos?'"

"These are both great examples. Now Myles and Jesse are going to write the answers to their partners' questions by adding to their stories. Jesse will write about who went to soccer practice with him, and Myles will explain where he played Legos.

"So, writers, take the questions you think your partner would ask, and answer their questions by finding a place to add words in, just like Myles and Jesse did. You might need to reread. Then start writing!"

I went to the bowling alley with my cousins. It was my birthday. I was turning six. It was in…

FIG. 6–1 Luka's story about going to the bowling alley where he added who he was with ("with my cousins")

Reading Our Writing Like We Read Our Books

IN THIS SESSION, you'll teach children that writers reread their own writing just like they read published books, making sure their writing is clear and makes sense for their readers.

GETTING READY

✔ Student who is the "teacher for the day." Set the child up by helping him find a piece of writing in his folder that he will reread in front of the class (see Connection).

✔ A pointer for the child to use when rereading his story, to point under each of his words

✔ Five or six students who will bring their writing to the minilesson where they will reread and fix up words that aren't quite right (see Teaching and Active Engagement)

✔ Children's folders, to be brought to the meeting area (see Active Engagement)

✔ Pencil or pen for each child to use in Active Engagement

✔ Students' first and most recent stories they wrote this year (see Share)

✔ Narrative Writing Checklists Grades 1 and 2 (see Share)

✔ Author's Gallery bulletin board with thumbtacks and a few pieces of construction paper to be used for headings on the board (see Share)

COMMON CORE STATE STANDARDS: W.1.3, W.1.5; RFS.1.1, RFS.1.2, RFS.1.3, RFS.1.4; SL.1.1; L.1.1, L.1.2.d,e

TODAY IS THE LAST DAY OF THE FIRST BEND in the road of this unit, making this a time for reflection. You and the children will want to look back at the work they did on the first day of this unit and the work they have been doing since to notice ways they have already begun to grow. Your hope is that your children are already coming to see the writing workshop as a time for them to get better, in ways that the whole world can see.

To start today's session, you'll emphasize the importance of writing for readers. You can say, "The stories you have been writing are so terrific that you *must* let your friends read what you are writing. At the end of today, let's make a museum in our classroom: you can put your writing on display, and then circle from one table to another, reading each others' stories." That should create momentum enough to lure children to do some of the preparation work.

"First it is important to make sure that others can read your writing. Today, I'm going to teach you that writers don't just write. Writers also read. Writers go from being the writer to being the reader—of their own stories." As you coach children to read their own writing, draw on all the language you use in the teaching of reading, and use the same words when you coach writers to reread their writing. This will reinforce your children's concepts of words, which most should have securely in place during reading time. But teaching for transference is important. As the child rereads her own writing, she is apt to notice omitted words and to say, "Oops, I forgot something." By all means, encourage her to add the missing word, to make the small changes, so the writing sounds right and makes sense.

Encourage children to also look at the letters they have written on the page and make sure they actually say the words the child intended to write. If a child has spelled *listen* as "LISN," that shows an effort to record every sound. This isn't a time to be hyper-concerned about perfect spelling, but it is helpful to channel children to check that they have represented most of the sounds in a word and spelled the words they know by heart correctly. Your session, then, begins as an invitation to reread in preparation for having readers, and assumes that writers are able to write and reread a story in a day, which means working with great energy and productivity, spurred on by the announcement that the day will end with a museum.

Reading Our Writing Like We Read Our Books

CONNECTION

Recruit children to join you in watching a classmate reread his writing. Ask partners to whisper about ways the writer is doing things that kids usually do during reading time.

"Writers, yesterday, I watched Jesse work on his writing, and for a moment I thought, 'Is this reading time or writing time?' Jesse was doing a *ton* of things that you guys do during *reading*. Will you and your partner team up and watch Jesse with me? He's going to do the same work that he was doing yesterday. I want you and your partner to whisper together whenever you see Jesse doing something that you do during *reading* time. It is like we'll all be spying on him!

"Okay, Jesse, will you do the work you did yesterday?"

Jesse got out the story he had written the previous day. He read the cover and the author's name, and then he turned to page 1. He looked at the picture and then read the words, pointing under each one with a pointer. Then he turned to page 2, looked at the picture, and again read, pointing. As Jesse worked, the children whispered.

Collect a list of ways that kids' work is similar whether they are reading from their books during reading workshop or rereading their own writing.

After Jesse finished reading two pages, I stopped him and asked children to help me gather a list of all the ways Jesse's work was the same as the reading work they do whenever they are reading during reading workshop.

Students responded with, "He looked at the picture and then read the words" and "He touched the words, one by one."

I nodded. "I saw the same things! What Jesse did is what all writers do."

♣ Name the teaching point.

"Writers, today I want to teach you that writers go from being the writer to being the reader. And when writers reread their own books, they read just as if they were reading a published book. And sometimes, the writer hears a mess-up and says, 'Oops,' and fixes that part."

For the connection today, you may decide to choose a student who is not as strong of a writer as some of the other children, both to boost his confidence and to emphasize the importance of working hard at our writing.

TEACHING

Set students up to research a classmate as he or she reads yesterday's writing.

"I've ask a few of you to bring your booklets from yesterday with you to the meeting area. Those of you who have your booklet with you, hold it up." Dotting the meeting area, five kids held their booklets high. "Will each of you show us what it is like when a writer becomes a reader, reading his or her own book, just like it was a published book?"

In a stage whisper to the class, I said, "Class, before the kids do this, let's remind ourselves of all the things we know that grown-up writers do when they reread their writing, so you can watch really closely and see if the writer near you does those things. And if not, you can remind him or her." I reiterated:

◆ Grown-up writers reread their writing the same way they read books.

◆ Grown-up writers read along until they come to mistakes, like words they left out, and then they say, "Oops," and fix it!

"You ready to study how writers becomes readers? We are going to watch writers together, and then we'll talk about what we noticed. Go ahead!"

After a few short moments, I said, "Observers, give a big thumbs up if you saw a writer pointing under words as he or she was reading them. How about a thumbs up if you saw a writer-reader reading the picture *and* the words! Has anyone seen a writer-reader say, 'Oops!' and fix something up?"

Debrief about the observations just made.

"When these writers read their writing, they transformed from a writer to a reader, and they used strategies we use when we read. Rereading helps writers make sure their stories make sense and helps them make sure that everything they need to say is there. Sometimes a writer also checks that their spelling is the best it can be."

ACTIVE ENGAGEMENT

Give children opportunities to be readers of their own writing.

"Now it is time for *all* of you to be the readers of your own writing. You are sitting on your writing folders. Take a minute and pick a story from your finished side that you want to read today. I'll give each of you a marker pen so you can fix up anything you notice that needs fixing up. Imagine your book is from reading workshop. Read it just like that."

While you will set students up to do the work of rereading and fixing up in the teaching, you will want to make sure to name out the strategies being demonstrated so the observing writers remain focused on the process their peers are going through rather than paying attention to the content of their classmate's stories.

LINK

Debrief in ways that remind children that they've now learned several things writers do when a piece is done and several ways to get ready to write.

"Writers, a few days ago we learned the saying 'When you are done, you've just begun.' And we learned that when you finish your writing, you can go back and add more to it. Do you remember that to get ideas for what to add, you can look at a picture you have drawn, remember the time you are writing about, and ask questions such as 'Who?' 'Where?' 'When?' 'What?' and 'How?' Today we learned one more thing you can do when you are done writing. You can shift to being a reader, and you can read your writing like you read books during reading workshop—only keeping a pen handy in case you find mess-ups.

"Right now, tell your partner whether you'll be starting a new book or continuing work on one, and if you are starting a new book, help each other touch and tell so that you are ready to write. Once you know what you'll be doing, you can go back to your seat and get started."

Helping Writers Use Spelling Strategies

A T THE CLOSE OF TODAY'S WRITING WORKSHOP, you're going to invite students to lay their writing out on tables as if the classroom is a museum and then to let others move from one table to the next, admiring the work. That's intended to provide a low-key audience, creating a minor sort of a culminating activity to mark the end of the first bend in the road of this unit and the start of the second. The fact that children will be sharing their writing with each other should make them extra willing to check that their writing is accessible to readers, making it timely for you to help them check their spelling.

You will probably want to lead a small group or two to encourage children to use the word wall to check that they have spelled sight vocabulary words correctly. Some writers will attempt to spell high-frequency words phonetically and will need to be reminded that there are some words they just know. Instead of sounding out *was* and *said*, for example, you'll want to encourage them to close their eyes and picture those words, relying on their visual memory of them. You may want to give those who need help moving from spelling phonetically toward spelling by sight-memory their own personal word walls. If these are kept in a plastic sleeve, they seem quite fancy, and the tool can lure youngsters to rely more on a visual memory of words. Whether you give youngsters their own word wall or rely on a class word wall, keep in mind that if you want children to use the word wall when writing, they need a lot of practice reading it so they can quickly locate a word. Some of this practice will happen during word study, outside of the writing workshop, but some of it can happen during conferences and small-group instruction within the writing workshop. You might, for example, start your small-group lesson by suggesting the children you convene read their personal copies of the word wall in unison, pointing under each word as they say it. If children are familiar with the words on the word wall, when they need to write a word that is on that list, rather than stretching the word out, they will know to either draw on their sight memory of it or check the word wall to renew that memory.

Meanwhile, teach children that when they've found a word they want to spell on the word wall, they need to look at that word, picturing the whole word in their mind, and

---

MID-WORKSHOP TEACHING Writers Are Readers of Their Own Writing, Fixing Words and Meaning as They Read

"So, writers, can I interrupt you for a minute?" I waited until children were looking at me. "Today is a special day. At the end of our workshop, instead of all of us coming to the carpet and having a meeting, are you up for turning this class into a museum? How many of you have been to or read about those museums that show dinosaur bones? In those museums, there are displays, and everyone walks around and admires the dinosaur bones. I'm thinking we could put your writing out on the table, and then your classmates could go around and admire your writing. Are you game to do this?" The children conveyed that yes, sure, they'd put their writing in a museum. I cautioned, "But to do this, you are going to want to make sure you fix up your writing so the kids can *read* it.

"Right now, with your partner, reread your writing just like Jesse read his story today, pointing together (two fingers) under the words. If you see something missing, say, 'Oops,' and then fix it."

---

then they should try to write the word without looking back. Of course, once the word is written, the writer will need to look back to the word wall to check the spelling.

You will probably also find that for some of your students, it is unclear whether they have spelled sight words correctly or not because the letters of most words are all smushed together, making the writing almost illegible. Often writers get so excited about hearing the sounds in their words that they go from one word to the next, forgetting to separate words with white spaces. Most of these writers have developed a concept of words when reading and, with help, can insert spaces between words when they write. Perhaps you'll pull these writers together and do a small-group interactive writing session to help them practice planning and writing sentences with spaces between each word. In such a group, you could bring out your own story on enlarged paper and ask them to help you add a sentence. Spend time touching and telling the sentence, hearing each word separately. You might ask them to put one finger up for each word in the agreed upon sentence, to count how many words they will write. You could ask them to clap the words, to jump for each word, or to draw blanks for each word. Then encourage them to say the sentence again, locating the first word, and then to say that word slowly while sliding a finger across the page. Then it will be time for the children in the small group to join you in hearing all the sounds in that first word. When there are no more sounds, ask one student to put a finger down to create a finger space before the next word.

Use the language you will use when you prompt them with their own writing. "Reread. Write the next word. No more sounds? Put a finger space," gesturing with your finger.

For children who need even more support with this, you may want to draw one line for each word and have them practice saying the words that will go on each line again and again. This way they learn that all the letters for one word go together and are separate from the letters of another word. Before ending the session, make sure to have students take out their own writing and give this a try. This way they transfer the learning from the interactive writing lesson to their own writing. Make sure they say and point to where each word will go on the page before they start writing.

While a great deal of your conferring time with writers will be in support of monitoring visual aspects of their writing (spelling, spacing), it is also important that our teaching encourages monitoring for sense and language structure as well. Therefore, after helping a writer fix up his spelling, encourage him to reread to make sure his writing makes sense and sounds like a book.

Celebrating Growth as Writers and Setting New Goals

Recruit children to help you set up the museum, selecting their best work, adding stickers or a quick border to it, and laying it alongside their very first piece of writing, to illuminate growth.

"Writers, it is time for our museum. Quick as a wink, clean up your writing spot and then put your best piece of writing on the table. I'm going to give you some stickers to put around the edge of it to pretty it up."

As children worked, I said, "Writers, I am coming around to hand you the *very* first piece you worked on this year. Put that out, too, and you and everyone else will have a chance to see how much you have grown as a writer." I turned on some fancy music, suggested children could browse from table to table, encouraging them to read the words, and told them they could draw a star or a smiley face on the top of any story they read and loved. "Notice how much your classmates have changed from the beginning of the year until now!" As children milled about, I cautioned, "Remember, museums are quiet as people study the exhibits. They are like libraries."

Channel children to self-assess their growth as narrative writers.

After some time, I asked the writers to go back to their pieces, hold them in front of them, and admire the readers' notes (stars and smiley faces). "Writers, look at the very first piece you wrote in first grade and look at the story you shared today. You've become better writers just in the short time we've been writing together! Look closely at your two stories. Find one thing that you do better now when you write. Give me a thumbs up when you know one way you have become a better writer.

"Writers, you are doing all that you learned in kindergarten and now you are starting to become more like first-grade writers. I think it is time to introduce a new Narrative Writing Checklist, one that shows all the goals you should be working toward this year as narrative writers and next year as second-grade narrative writers too. These are the things that hundreds of adults decided first- and second-graders should be able to do by the end of each year. So, you won't be doing all of these things just yet, but many of them you will be." I read the list. (The Narrative Writing Checklist, Grades 1 and 2 is available on the CD-ROM.)

"Look at your best piece, the one you shared today, and think about what on this list you already do as a writer. I'll read each one again. Give me thumbs up if you did the work in your story. Writers, you've become such strong writers even in this first week of first grade! Turn and tell your partner what you have learned to do *now* that you didn't do just a week or two ago. Remember to think about that first piece and the story you shared today.

"Now turn and ask your partner how he or she has become a better writer." I walked between partnerships, listening in and jotting notes. "I added details. Here I put more about where I was," said Myles as he lifted the flap on his page. "Me too," said his partner, Emma. "I wrote more words on the page." "I added some here on the last page," announced Marco proudly. "In my first story," Emma said, "I wrote about all the things I did at my friend's house—a watermelon story. Now I'm an even better writer because I wrote *just* about the nail place." (See Figures 7–1 and 7–2.)

"Writers we all have become better writers. Some of us are writing our words with more letters so other people can read them easily." I wrote, "I used all I know about words to help me spell" on a small piece of construction paper and put it on the section of our Author's Gallery bulletin board. "Other writers are the kind of writers who go back to their writing when they think they are done and add more details to their pictures or words." I wrote, "I added more details" on another piece of paper. "Some writers used to write watermelon stories and are now writing small seed stories." I wrote, "I wrote about *one time* when I did something" on another piece of paper and pinned it to another section of the bulletin board.

"Okay, writers, I've put up these ways you are becoming better writers on our Author's Gallery. This is where we will be sharing some of your writing pieces throughout the school year. Some of your writing will go here, and some of the books you write will go in our classroom library. This way we can read and enjoy each other's writing like we read the books in our classroom. This month when anyone comes in our room we can show them how you have grown as writers by putting your stories on the bulletin board according to your accomplishments and the kinds of writers you are! Right now think about where your writing will go. Which kind of writer are you? Let's start with writers who now write seed stories about *one time* they did something instead of watermelon stories. Come on up with your story!" A few writers came up to the Author's Gallery, and I helped them place their writing on the board. We clapped as the writers went back to their tables. I did the same with the other two sections: "I used all I know about words to help me spell" and "I added details."

We clapped as the final story was added to the Author's Gallery. "Writers, congratulations! Now everyone will see the exciting work we've been doing already in our writing workshop!"

Narrative Writing Checklist

	Kindergarten	NOT YET	STARTING TO	YES!	Grade 1	NOT YET	STARTING TO	YES!
	Structure				**Structure**			
Overall	I told, drew, and wrote a whole story.	☐	☐	☐	I wrote about when I did something.	☐	☐	☐
Lead	I had a page that showed what happened first.	☐	☐	☐	I tried to make a beginning for my story.	☐	☐	☐
Transitions	I put my pages in order.	☐	☐	☐	I put my pages in order. I used words such as *and* and *then, so*.	☐	☐	☐
Ending	I had a page that showed what happened last in my story.	☐	☐	☐	I found a way to end my story.	☐	☐	☐
Organization	My story had a page for the beginning, a page for the middle, and a page for the end.	☐	☐	☐	I wrote my story across three or more pages.	☐	☐	☐
	Development				**Development**			
Elaboration	My story indicated who was there, what they did, and how the characters felt.	☐	☐	☐	I put the picture from my mind onto the page. I had details in pictures and words.	☐	☐	☐
Craft	I drew and wrote some details about what happened.	☐	☐	☐	I used labels and words to give details.	☐	☐	☐
	Language Conventions				**Language Conventions**			
Spelling	I could read my writing.	☐	☐	☐	I used all I knew about words and chunks of words (*at, op, it*, etc.) to help me spell.	☐	☐	☐
	I wrote a letter for the sounds I heard.	☐	☐	☐	I spelled all the word wall words right and used the word wall to help me spell other words.	☐	☐	☐
	I used the word wall to help me spell.	☐	☐	☐				

Page 1: I went to my friend Amanda's house.   Page 2: Then we watched TV.   Page 3: Then I went home and ate dinner.

FIG. 7–1   Emma's first story, a "watermelon" story, in which she told about the whole day

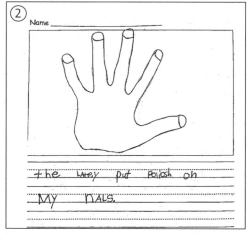

Page 1: We went to the nail place.   Page 2: The lady put polish on my nails.   Page 3: I said "thank you." My nails were pretty.

FIG. 7–2   Emma's story after she reread, focused on one small moment, and stretched it out across pages

I take a bath bubble bath. I like
to take a bath. Mommy let me
do it.

I got out of the tub.
I put on my princess pajamas.

I brush my teeth.

I go to sleep. It was good.

FIG. 7–3 Kidiamary's story about getting ready for bed. Kidiamary focuses on one event, writing actions in sequence that match her pictures and sentences, which she added when her partner asked her questions to revise.

 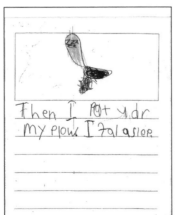  

One day I was eating an apple.
Then my tooth got loose.

Then I put it under my pillow.
I fell asleep.

Then the tooth fairy came
to get my tooth.

And she gave me a dollar.

FIG. 7–4 Angelina's "seed" story (rather than "watermelon" story) about losing a tooth, which she begins to develop with details like the speech bubble (in which she writres, "I was happy") and makes changes to words after rereading her writing (e.g., *put* to which she adds a *u* over the *o*).

I can ride my skateboard with Ray.   I can do tricks.   I can play in the park.

FIG. 7–5   Taivaun's skateboarding story shows his approximation of writing a seed story. In this Taivaun writes two out of three pages about one event before switching to another story.

Unfreezing Our Characters and Our Writing

IN THIS SESSION, you'll teach children how writers bring their stories to life by making their characters move and speak.

GETTING READY

✔ Your own story with very little detail in the drawings: stick figures, no setting, simple sentences that just list what was happening on each page. (You will probably want to save this piece to use in the realistic fiction unit.)

✔ Chart paper and markers, to create a new class chart, "Ways to Bring Stories to Life" (see Active Engagement)

✔ Blank booklet and pen or pencil for each student, to be brought to the meeting area

✔ Sample first-grade story that includes dialogue (see Mid-Workshop Teaching)

✔ Your own skill Post-it book and extra Post-its to make reminder Post-its for children during conferring and small-group work (optional)

COMMON CORE STATE STANDARDS: W.1.3, W.2.3; RL.1.1, RL.1.3; SL.1.1, SL.1.4, SL.1.5; L.1.1, L.1.2

W HEN YOUNG CHILDREN ARE FIRST READING chapter books, the ending of one chapter and the start of a new one is an especially helpful structure. These markers say to the young reader, "You've come a long way. Congratulations. Now you are ready for another challenge!" The ending of one bend in a unit and the start of the next one can function in a similar way to young writers. Today, then, is an occasion. It is the start of the second bend in the journey of this unit. Because children may not have the same connection as you and I have to the image of a bend in the road, you may choose to describe this new section of the unit as Part Two or Chapter Two. The words you use to describe this demarcation are not important; what is important is that you let children in on the fact that today is the start of a whole new part of the unit.

It'll be necessary, then, to draw a line between the work children have been doing so far and the new work they'll begin doing today. The truth is that there will be many ways their work is the same. They've been cranking out tons of little, focused personal narratives, and they'll continue to do so. They've been touching the pages of a book, saying aloud the story they plan to write, and then sketching and writing that story, and they'll continue to do so. They've been tapping into all they know about spelling and phonics and sight words to spell as best they can, without getting themselves tied in knots over an obsessive worry about perfection, and they'll continue to do that work. But for now, you won't emphasize the fact that in many ways the ongoing work of the unit is the same. Instead, for now, you'll emphasize the way this unit is reaching toward a new and higher goal. So you will see that today's lesson tries to rally kids to write in ways that bring stories to life. You are helping children aspire to make the people in their stories come to life and walk right off the page.

In the minilessons that follow across this bend, you are going to teach kids specific ways to make their stories come to life. The content of your teaching will reach toward the second-grade skills on the narrative learning progression. For example, the learning progression suggests that in first grade, children learn to bring flavor to their writing through elaboration, and the elaboration involves writing with detail. You'll help them do this—using direct dialogue and including characters' actions, thoughts, and feelings. By second grade students are expected to elaborate by writing with detail, talk, and action.

In the end, this bend in the road is an effort for you to convey to children that writing well means thinking not only about *what you say*, but also about *how you say it*. You'll be making an effort to move writers from chronicling the sequence of what happened toward storytelling that sequence. You'll be encouraging writers to think about their readers and to do everything possible to help readers picture how the characters looked and how the setting felt.

"You are helping children aspire to make the people in their stories come to life and walk right off the page."

You will begin this bend by teaching children that for a story to be lively—for it to jump off the pages and into a reader's imagination—the people need to do things. They need to move and talk. Chances are many of your children have been writing stories in which not much happens. "I went to McDonalds. It was good. Yum, yum." "My Dad came home. I missed him. I am happy." Today's teaching aims to help students "unfreeze" their characters by giving them actions and voices, too.

Adding dialogue may translate into one- or two-word speech bubbles for many of your students and longer quotations for others. It is well within reach of most first-graders to tell what they did, what the people did, in the story. The Common Core State Standards call for first-graders to be able to write narratives in which they recount two or more appropriately sequenced events, including some details regarding what happened. This day's work supports, and reaches beyond, that goal.

Children will benefit from exposure to stories that are full of precise, obvious actions. That is, in addition to introducing your students to more books that brim with beautiful language, you'll want to be sure children are also hearing and reading plenty of stories in which characters are active agents—stories in which goats tromp across bridges, kids run away from home, friends fight—that is, stories in which things happen.

Unfreezing Our Characters and Our Writing

CONNECTION

◆ COACHING

Tell children about a story you wrote, and then explain that upon rereading it, you realized your characters were "frozen."

"Writers, I started a new story about the fire drill that happened last week. Remember how the alarm went off, and then we lined up, and then we walked down the warm hall, and then we pushed open the door and suddenly it was so cold. We were hopping up and down to keep warm.

"Look! I wrote the first three pages already." I turned to an enlarged booklet and read from a page with stick figure drawings only. "I heard the fire bell." Then I turned to the next page, with equally underdeveloped stick figures, and read, "I lined up with the class." Again I turned the page to reveal the same lifeless figures, now standing in the hall. "We walked down the hall."

"Huh. That's funny. My story doesn't sound like the books we've been reading. It's sorta flat. And not much happens. I bet people who weren't here will have no idea what our fire drill was *really* like. They won't know that Pedro went scurrying around the room looking for Magic, who slipped out of his arms when the bell startled them both, or that we were all trying to be really calm and quiet and using our one-inch voices to talk.

"Look at my pictures of you guys," I said and pointed to the line of stick figures, all standing with legs straight, arms outstretched, featureless. "You're all so still. And look at me, just standing, with my arms at my sides! My face doesn't even change, does it? And look at this, too. The alarm is going off but none of us are even saying anything!

"You know how in the game of freeze tag, when you touch people and say 'Freeze!' they aren't allowed to move or say anything? Well, it's like all the people in the start of my story are frozen. I wrote what happened—we heard the alarm, we lined up—but I didn't show what we said or did."

❖ **Name the teaching point.**

"Today I want to teach you that just like published writers, you can make your stories come to life. You can 'unfreeze' the people in your stories by making them move," I moved my arms like I was running, "and talk." I opened and closed my hand almost like a puppet talking.

I am demonstrating by writing (and revising) publicly. It is almost as if I take the top off my head and let children see the wheels in my brain turn. But, of course, the strategies I spotlight for kids aren't necessarily those that I actually use as I (as an adult) write and revise. Instead I demonstrate and highlight strategies I see as within grasp of the kids.

TEACHING

Show children the underdeveloped story you've written, containing little or no action or dialogue.

"Let me show you what I mean. Listen again to the way our fire drill story goes so far." I read off the chart:

> I heard the fire bell.
> I lined up with the class.
> We walked down the hall.

Demonstrate how you go about bringing the characters to life by recalling what happened and writing in more detail.

"Now let's see if we can bring this story to life! Let's unfreeze the people. Hmm, the little actions we have so far are not that active. There's no real movement, and no talking at all!

"Let's see," I mused and then said, "I didn't just *hear* the fire bell. I was *startled* by it. That bell was loud. It made me jump. I've got to get that in. And someone else got a little scared, too—our poor rabbit, Magic! Okay, how about this?" I read the revised story with expression, emphasizing the movement.

> CLANG, CLANG, CLANG went the bell. I JUMPED. Magic SLIPPED out of Pedro's arms and
> SCURRIED under a desk.

"Thumbs up if you think that's a more exciting, active beginning than 'I heard the fire bell.'" Lots of eager thumbs went up.

"Now, as soon as I heard the bell, was I totally silent? Did I signal for you all to meet me at the door? No way! I called all of you to line up. So let's get that into the story. Let's write exactly what I *said* to you."

> Clang, clang, clang went the bell. I jumped. Magic slipped out of Pedro's arms and scurried
> under a desk.
> "Everyone, quickly line up at the door!" I called out.

ACTIVE ENGAGEMENT

Rally students to continue with the next part of the story, working with partners to bring the story to life.

"Will you take over now? Remember what happened next and try to think what words we can use to unfreeze the people—to show how we moved, what our faces looked like, what we said. Do you remember how all of you guys lined

Be sure your selected small moment is an ordinary one to which children can relate. While a shared class experience works best, as students can easily add on to the story during the active engagement, you could also write about other small moments. Perhaps when it was time to go to school you couldn't find your shoe—looked all over—and found it in a weird place. Or perhaps you were making cookies and didn't have an ingredient so you substituted something different and it turned out awful, or okay.

up, except Pedro who was crawling around after Magic? Will Partner 1 please write in the air, telling Partner 2 what you would write next?" As children talked, I listened.

Recruit the children to help you add onto the class story, and then reread it, emphasizing what students have just done that they can do again in another piece.

"Eyes up here." I waited until I had their attention. "Who can help us put some more into our story? Pedro, what do you think we should say next?" Soon our story looked like this.

> Clang, clang, clang went the bell. I jumped. Magic slipped out of Pedro's arms and scurried under a desk.
> "Everyone, quickly line up at the door!" I called out.
> Most kids got in line. Pedro was crawling around on the floor, looking for Magic. "Hurry," we said to him.
> Finally, we were all ready to walk down the hall. We used our one-inch voices.

I read the story aloud, with great expression and then said, "Writers, do you see how adding in the things we *did* and *said* brought this first part of the story to life? Now if anyone were to read our story about the fire drill, they'd be able to picture it in their minds, reliving the excitement of that event with us."

Introduce the chart "Ways to Bring Stories to Life."

"Over the next week or so, we're going to be learning lots of ways to liven up our stories like this. I want all of you to have little reminders as you write. Let's begin a new chart and call it 'Ways to Bring Stories to Life.' I wrote the title. "So our first way will be . . . " I let my voice trail off and gestured to the children to fill in the missing information. They called out in unison, "Unfreeze the people!"

You will want to decide how you will create the chart with the students. One way is to have strategy cards created ahead of time to add to the chart as the strategies are introduced. You may decide to have the words prewritten and add a picture or symbol in front of the children.

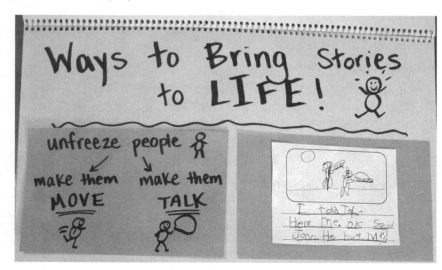

LINK

Channel children to think of the story they will write today and create a picture that helps them start the story well.

"In a minute, you are going to go and write your own stories. Before you head off, think of an idea for your next story. It might help to think of a time when you had a strong feeling and a time you really remember well so that you can do what we have done, and remember the little details that make the moment come to life. Thumbs up when you have an idea for a new story.

"Now think. Where were you? Do you remember? Close your eyes. Thumbs up if you can picture it.

"Now keep thinking. Who else was there? What did they look like? Thumbs up if you can picture them.

"Now try to remember the first thing that happened. Were you just standing there, with your arms out at your sides, saying nothing?" I made myself into a stick figure. "Try to remember exactly how you were walking or running, or sitting or standing. Try to remember what you might have said. When you remember, give a thumbs up.

"Great. Now, everybody, start sketching the first page of your story, right now, while you are sitting here.

"Remember that you already learned that it helps to plan out your whole story, sketching out all the pages. Then you can go back and write the words. Only now, the difference is that you won't just write what happened. You'll write in a way that makes your story comes to life."

Helping Children Write with Greater Volume and Detail

THE WORK OF TODAY'S SESSION sets students up to write more down the page, filling their lines with more details than they ever have before. Although many of your children will have moved into writing more and drawing less, you will notice that some writers continue to write only one sentence on a page, telling their story through the details in their pictures instead. These children are often the writers who spend so much time drawing intricate pictures that they don't have much time left for writing. They will need your support in moving away from drawing in detail to writing more detail in words. For some writers this may mean teaching them to write the dialogue

---

MID-WORKSHOP TEACHING   Writers Have Ways to Get People in Stories to Talk

"Writers, eyes on me please!" I waited until I had the kids' attention. "I just saw Sekou doing the *coolest* thing. He had sketched all his pages, just like we learned last week, and he was touching each page to say what would go there, but he added his own little twist. As he touched the people in the pictures, he made them talk. I sat down next to him and listened to the way he was telling his story. It was as if the people in the sketches were talking to each other, back and forth, right there on the page. I turned to the second page of Sekou's story and asked him to make the people talk, and then did the same for the third page. Then, when he wrote the story, he wrote what each person said." (See Figure 8–1.)

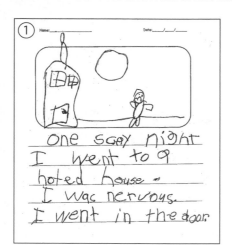

FIG. 8–1   Sekou's story about going to a haunted house in which he made the characters move and talk even before he wrote the words

Page 1: One scary night I went to a haunted house. I was nervous. I went in the door.

Page 2: The big vampire bat and mummy jumped. I yelled, "Help!" I ran and ran.

Page 3: I told John, "Help me." "OK," said John. He hugged me!

"I thought, 'Wow! What a cool way to make your story come to life!'"

"Well that got me thinking, writers. What better way to make your characters come to life than to make them talk, even before you write! Sekou tapped his pictures each time a person spoke, and you can try that too. Or you could even use your hands to be the people, like puppets." I held up each hand and made little cupping motions to indicate puppets. "Sekou, pretend with me. Ready?" I held up my wiggling fingers. "Hello, Sekou," I said, in a silly pretend voice, tapping him on the shoulder with my right cupped hand. Sekou giggled until I tapped him again, indicating that he should respond.

"Um, hi," he said, holding up his cupped hand.

"What a clever idea, Sekou," I said, making my hand match his. "You've taught us all a way to wake up our people!"

Then, resuming my role as teacher, I said, "Writers, you may want to try Sekou's strategy and touch your pictures so they talk. Or you may want to make hand puppets or use your pens as the characters and get them talking to each other. Try it, for now. Partner 2, try touching a person in your picture to make that person talk, and then touch the other person and have him or her talk back. Anyone who wants to use pens to do their talking, hold up your pen now and get started."

After children did this for a little while, I said, "Writers, now the challenge is to put those voices onto the pages of your stories. Do that now."

in the pictures through speech bubbles. This is a more concrete way to make the characters talk that they probably learned in kindergarten. You can show them how they touch a person in the picture, say what the person said, write the words next to the person, and then draw a bubble around the words. Other writers need support with sketching so that more time is available for writing. This is not easy for some writers at first, because we have to teach them to determine importance and then find ways to draw in a quick and simple way. If this description fits some of your students, you may decide to pull a group of writers who need more support with writing with greater volume and detail into a strategy group.

During any strategy group, you will draw on your observations to bring together students who need practice on the same skill or who need to be pushed in similar ways to try something new. As in a minilesson, there will be a connection, teaching point, teaching, active engagement, and link in your strategy lesson; however, these elements will all be abbreviated, and most of the time will be devoted to children actually trying out the strategy while you coach into their work.

First, pull the students into a semicircle around you on the rug so that they can see and hear you. Your connection will be very brief, stating why you have pulled these particular students together. "I have brought you together because I noticed that you are putting so much detail into your drawings! You are all spending *so* much time on your drawings, though, and I am worried you are not getting enough time to write words! Remember that writers use both pictures *and* words to tell their stories." Then, immediately after that, name your teaching point, "Today I want to teach you a special kind of drawing that writers use when they want to save time for writing. You've heard it before. It's called *sketching*. You can quickly sketch just the important stuff, without all the fancy details, so you can get straight to writing words."

Your demonstration will again be brief, because the important part is to get the students working on their own pieces. "Watch me as I sketch our class story about the time our class had the fire drill. Notice how I sketch without all the fancy details, so I can get straight to writing words. First, I will do what we will always do in here. I will touch the page and say what I will write. The fire bell clanged and we all lined up. Now I am going to take my pencil and sketch what happened on the page." I quickly sketched the class lining up at the staircase, using only the outline shapes of people and surroundings. "Did you notice how I am not even giving the people hair or little details, like shoelaces? I am not adding all of the beautiful bulletin boards in the hallway. I can add all those details later."

During the active engagement, mobilize students to sketch and write their own pieces, perhaps with partner support, setting them up much as you do during the active engagement sections of a minilesson. "Now it's your turn to try this with your stories.

I want you to think of your story, touch each page, and say what's happening. Then make a quick sketch." Once the children are working on this, you will move from student to student, spending only a few seconds to notice what they are doing and coach into their work with quick prompts, saying, "Wow!" or "Not too fancy, just a quick sketch!"

You will want to make it around to each student two or three times, turning your body around the semicircle and doling out quick prompts. At this point, you may want to leave the group so they can continue working at the rug while you pull other groups or have one-to-one conferences. When you return to the group after six or seven minutes, wrap it up with a brief link. "So, writers, remember that every day, when you are planning your stories, you can sketch without all the fancy details so you can get straight to writing words." You may want to leave each writer with a physical representation of their learning, such as a Post-It with a picture and word or phrase that will serve as a reminder while they write. (See Figures 8–2 and 8–3.) Then send the children back to their seats to work independently.

FIG. 8–2   One child's reminder Post-it that is stored on the inside of the writer's folder and then taken out during writing time and set on the table or desk

FIG. 8–3   A teacher's skill Post-It book, each page with a set of Post-Its ready to be given out to students in conferences or small groups as a physical represenation of what they are learning and should be practicing while writing

Letting Readers Know When Someone Is Talking

Teach children the purpose of quotation marks, guiding them to think about their reader.

"Writers, your stories are really coming to life! It's been so much fun peering over your shoulders and discovering all the actions you're putting onto the page and reading what the people in your stories are saying. I want to tell you about something that will help with the talking parts. When writers write dialogue (that means the words people say) in their stories, there is a special mark they use to show that these are the words coming from the person. They look like this." I drew them on a piece of chart paper. "You write the first quotation mark right before the first word the person says, and then you write the ending quotation mark right after the last word the person says. Notice how the first quotation mark curls in to the right toward the first word and the second one curls in to the left toward the last word. The quotation marks wrap the dialogue. That way the reader can tell when someone is speaking.

"Just like we know to stop when we come to a period mark, quotation marks are there to tell the reader that the words inside are the words the person is saying. The marks give readers a hint. It's like they're saying, 'Change your voice, someone is talking!'"

Recruit children to reread their writing and add quotation marks to places where people speak. Then channel them to read their writing aloud, using intonation to make the dialogue come to life.

"Writers, try this now. First, reread your story and put a right-curling quotation mark right before the first word of the person talking, and put a left-curling quotation mark right after the last word the person says.

"Now turn and read your story to your partner, changing your voice when you get to the words in quotation marks. If it is your mom reminding you yet again to clean your room, make your voice sound grumpy. If it is you saying something when you are scared, make your voice sound shaky and little. If it is your soccer coach calling out directions to the team, make your voice really big and authoritative.

"Great work, writers! I heard lots of voices for the different people in your stories. Remember, when you add dialogue to make your stories come to life, you put quotation marks around the words people say so the reader knows to change his or her voice."

Telling Stories in Itsy-Bitsy Steps

IN THIS SESSION, you'll teach children that writers bring their stories to life by unfolding the action bit by bit.

GETTING READY

✔ Be prepared to sing "The Itsy-Bitsy Spider" during the connection. You will use the song to explain how stories move across the page in little steps.

✔ "Ways to Bring Stories to Life" chart, to add to after the teaching point

✔ Mentor text, *Night of the Veggie Monster* (or any picture book that has a stretched-out small moment and that children know well) (see Teaching)

✔ The start of a class story that children will help tell during the active engagement, aiming to do so in small steps

✔ Your own not-yet-written story to demonstrate how to plan for a story, telling it across your fingers bit by bit, saying more at each finger (see Share)

COMMON CORE STATE STANDARDS: W.1.3, W.1.5; RL.1.1; SL.1.1, SL.1.4, SL.1.5; L.1.1, L.1.2

I F YOUR CHILDREN'S WRITING doesn't match your fire drill story, don't be surprised. It's a very big deal to teach children to write in such a way that the story sparkles with vitality. If many of your children's stories feel bland, almost as if they are lists of actions rather than small dramas, one of the things you will want to think about is whether you can create more opportunities for storytelling within the school day. If you have snack time, for example, listen as your children talk to each other. Chances are they will be talking about the here and now—about their chips, the sandwich, the chair—and not re-creating events that occurred in another time and place, regaling each other with stories of their baby brother or their dog. Shirley Brice Heath, one of the nation's foremost researchers of children's language development, suggests that there is a close relationship between children's abilities to spin their lives into oral stories and their abilities to succeed in school. She encourages parents to value storytelling. Think about it. How often do you hear a parent luring a child to retell, with enormous detail, the events that occurred during recess or during the bus ride?

If you have an opportunity to meet with your parents and to encourage them to create opportunities for children to story-tell at home, by all means do so. But whether or not you can influence parents, you can certainly think about your school day and build in more times for children to tell each other the small stories of their lives. Why not start every morning with small storytelling circles. Instead of a formal whole-class show and tell time where one child pulls an action figure from his or her pocket and shows it to the lustful other children, you could organize your classroom so that half a dozen children bring in something—a sketch, an object—that holds a story and then tell that story with enormous detail and drama. After recess, children can pull together into storytelling circles, and one child can tell a story of what occurred during recess. This emphasis on building a rich storytelling culture in your classroom will have a transformative effect on your children's writing.

As children talk and write, you'll want to continue teaching them about the characteristics of effective stories, and that instruction will be influenced by the narrative learning progression and specifically by the expectations for first-grade writers' progress from listing what happened first, next, then, and last to being able to recount stories through a series of small steps writing more than just a line or two on each page.

"An emphasis on building a rich storytelling culture in your classroom will have a transformative effect on your children's writing."

Your goal today will be for children to get a feel for the pacing of stories, to grasp that the most successful, satisfying stories are told in smallish steps, not in summary. With work, children will write, "I woke up and jumped out of bed. Then I ate breakfast. I told my mom I loved her. Then the bus came and took me to school." Such a story would be absolutely fine for a first-grader, although you can channel children to write with even more detail, slowing themselves down even more, telling more about what happened on each page before moving to the next episode in the story.

Think of today's teaching as introducing the concept of writing with more detail and elaboration, but don't expect children's stories to suddenly become extremely detailed. Just as you teach children to write bit by bit, so too will they learn bit by bit.

Telling Stories in Itsy-Bitsy Steps

CONNECTION

Recall and sing the famous children's song "The Itsy-Bitsy Spider" with the class.

"Writers, do you remember that song you learned last year about the spider climbing up the water spout? You do? Show me with your fingers how you make that spider climb. Let's sing it together. Get your fingers ready!" I said, getting my own two hands into position.

The children and I made our fingers climb an imaginary water spout as we sang, "The itsy-bitsy spider climbed up the water spout. Down came the rain and washed the spider out. Out came the sun and dried up all the rain. And the itsy-bitsy spider climbed up the spout again."

When we were done, I said, "That is one of my favorite songs! I can really picture that spider in my mind. I can see those spider legs inching up, up, up, in itsy-bitsy movements." I gestured with my fingers again to show how the spider moves.

Sometimes a connection helps children recall past work and connect it to the day's new teaching. Sometimes, though, like today, it mainly serves as an attention-getter and/or a metaphor for the day's new teaching. If we'd started in directly with the teaching point, chances are most children would not be in the right frame of mind yet and would miss it.

Name the teaching point.

"Good stories are a lot like that spider. They take small steps. Today I want to teach you that when writers want to write stories that come to life on the page, they tell their stories in small steps, bit by bit. Writers think about the main thing they did and then ask themselves, 'What exactly happened, step by step, bit by bit?'"

I added the strategy "tell small steps" to the class chart.

Ways to Bring Stories to Life

- "Unfreeze" people—make them move, make them talk
- Tell small steps

TEACHING

Highlight how your mentor author stretched out a small moment, rereading that part of the text.

"Right now, think about what you would say if you were writing a story about your supper, and you didn't like some of your food but you ate it anyway." I gave children a little silence to think about that. "Maybe I'd write, 'I didn't want to eat the asparagus but I had to so I did.'

"But writers, the thing I have learned is that the real pro writers often take something as small as eating food you don't like, and they stretch the story out, writing it bit by bit. You remember one of our favorite books about the little boy who freaks out when he has to eat vegetables. Listen as I reread the part about him eating a pea. As I read, notice how long George McClements makes this one moment last, how slooooowly he stretches it out."

With just the slightest touch . . .

. . . it begins.

My fingers become all wiggly.

As the pea rests in my mouth, my eyes begin to WATER.

My toes twist and curl up in my shoes.

I SQUIRM in my seat. I try to keep control but the pea is too strong. I start to transform into . . .

. . . a VEGGIE MONSTER!

Ready to smash the chairs!

Ready to tip the table!

Ready to . . .

. . . GULP!

I swallowed the pea.

I actually swallowed the pea.

It tasted all right, really.

"Wow. All that buildup to eat just one pea! George McClements could have just written, 'I didn't want to eat the pea but then I did and it was okay.' But instead, he wrote it bit by bit."

Think aloud to the class about *how* the author might have stretched the moment out.

"So let's think about *how* he did this. I bet he looked at his sketch and remembered that time, and then he asked himself, 'What happened exactly, step by step?'

As you read aloud this part of the mentor text, draw out the drama to drive home the point. Kids will enjoy listening—and they'll understand the teaching behind the performance.

"He probably remembered one time when he was a kid who was forced to eat icky things, and sitting right there at his desk, it was probably almost like the disgusting food was right in front of him. Even though he was writing a story, not eating, he probably went," and I made my body revolt at imagined food as I said, "Ick! Then he probably remembered how it went and story-told that to himself. 'My fingers become all wiggly. My eyes begin to water. My toes twist and curl up, I squirm in my seat.' And then he was ready to write it all down.

"Writers, I saw some of you squirming on the rug just now. There was some toe curling, too. It was like all of you guys became that kid! That's what happens when you write or hear a story that moves in itsy-bitsy steps."

ACTIVE ENGAGEMENT

Recruit children to help construct a detailed story about their arrival at school that morning. Channel them to say aloud what they'd write to partners and contribute to a class story.

"So let's try this together. How about if you guys help me write about this morning when you came to school. How about it? I'll write, 'Today, lots of kids showed up at school. Then school started and later everyone went home. The end.' Does that sound like a good story?"

"No!" the kids called out.

"No?!" I made a sad face and then quickly recovered with "Hmm. That's one *big* step of a story. I want to tell my story in *itsy-bitsy* steps, like the spider. Let's see. Oh! I know. We need to recall exactly what happened, bit by bit. Turn and talk to your partner. Try to recall the little things that happened this morning."

I gave the children a minute to talk, and then I called out, "Put a thumb on your knee if you have something you want to share."

I called on Steven, who said, "I was the first kid in the room! And you told me my shirt with palm trees reminded you of Hawaii."

I smiled and gave him a thumbs up.

Jane said, "I came in and we had morning meeting."

"Think itsy-bitsy spider, Jane. Smaller, slower steps. What happened when you came in the room?"

"Umm, oh! You told me where to put my bag, and then you helped me get it in cause it was almost too big. We had to push it together to make it fit!"

I laughed. "That's more like it!"

Bring all the details children have suggested into a brief narrative of the morning, and then use this to debrief.

"Writers, we are ready to story-tell now. I'm going to take all your suggestions and see if I can get them all in."

> This morning, Stephen was the first to walk in. He came wearing a shirt with palm trees on it. "Great shirt, Stephen!" I said to him. "It reminds me of Hawaii." Jane came in with a bag almost as big as her. She tried to shove it into her cubby but it wouldn't fit. The two of us pushed and pushed until we squeezed it in.

"Does that sound like a more stretched-out story?" I asked, and the children nodded. "See how much I wrote, and I'm barely past the first ten minutes of today? That's what it means to write in itsy-bitsy steps."

LINK

Reiterate that writers inch through their stories, telling them bit by bit, and then send writers off to write.

"Everyone, show me your itsy-bitsy spider hands." I held mine up too. "Before you work on your own stories, I want to remind you that writers take their time when they write. They inch their stories across the page in itsy-bitsy steps. Some of you may be planning a new story today. As you do so, remember to sketch your story in little steps. If you're in the middle of a plan and it's moving too quickly, go ahead and add pages to your booklet. You know where the paper is. And those of you who are in the middle of writing, you might want to reread to be sure you're telling your story bit by bit, not in a big rush. Off you go, Writers!"

You will want to make sure in many of your links to acknowledge that writers are all in different parts of the process and provide a quick explanation of how this strategy can look in those different stages of the process. This way you are reminding writers to pick up where they left off and helping them to see how the work of the day's minilesson fits into the larger work of the unit.

Supporting Elaboration

Y OU'LL WANT TO MAKE SURE THAT YOUR CONFERRING addresses not just the teaching point from today, but all of the work you have taught thus far—plus any new challenges you see before you. If you find, for example, that yesterday's emphasis on recalling and adding in details needs more reinforcement, which is likely, you might gather a small group of youngsters and ask them to join you in helping one child, as I do below with Pedro.

I held the narrative learning progression next to my conferring notebook as I was conferring with Pedro. I looked to the learning progression to help me assess what he needed and to inform my teaching for the conference. I realized Pedro needed to write with detail, because this is one of the learning progression's goals for first-grade students. Instead of a one-on-one conference, I recruited five students who could also get stronger at writing with detail to help Pedro make his bare-bones story more detailed. By participating in the coaching aspect of the conference, the other writers get practice doing the work that they can then translate to their own writing.

I said to the group, "Let's see if we can help Pedro write his story in a way that makes his characters come to life. So far, he's written":

> I watched TV. I ate pizza.

"To make a story come to life, we need to be able to picture it in our minds. So, Pedro, can you tell us all about what you were doing when you watched TV, so that we can picture this in our minds? Come on up here and tell us about it."

Pedro shrugged. "That's all I did: watch TV," he said.

I nodded, "I can picture it. You stood in front of the TV . . ."

Pedro protested. "Nope. I lay in front of the TV. On my alligator. (That's what we call our huge green pillow.) And I watched *The Magic School Bus*."

MID-WORKSHOP TEACHING
Writers Act Out and Tell Bit by Bit

"Can I interrupt you for a moment, writers? Turn to one part of your story, a part where something really big happens—the important part—and remember back to that time. Put yourself in that place. Picture exactly what you did first in that part. Now, stand up and act that out.

"Go back to the beginning of that action. What were your hands doing? What were your legs doing? Where were you looking? Now, quickly, picture what you did next. Now, Partner 1, touch the page and tell Partner 2 *exactly* what you were doing and saying and thinking. Partner 2, help your partner go back and write about each small action, stretching the part out, filling up lots of lines on the page. Work together."

As Students Continue Working . . .

"Try asking yourselves, 'What came right after this?' each time you go to sketch or write another part of your story. And if your characters go galloping through the story instead of inching their way along, stop, go back, and add any bits you might have forgotten."

"Writers, remember that we put new words on the word wall this week so we can use them when we read *and* when we write! When you are trying to spell any of these words we are learning, make sure to find the word on the word wall, picture the whole word in your mind, and then write it down in a snap!"

"Aha. Yes, I see that big green alligator pillow, and I see you sprawled on it. Was anyone with you?"

"My brother, but he kept changing the channel and I got *so mad.*"

"Well, you weren't frozen at all, then! I'm picturing what a mad boy might do. Are you, too, writers?" The rest of the children nodded. "Tell your partner what angry Pedro might do as he lay there on his alligator pillow in front of the TV."

I heard the kids say things like, "He'd grab the remote" and "He'd punch the alligator pillow."

I said to the children, "Let's all of us think about how we could help Pedro make his characters come to life. No frozen characters this time. We're going to want his characters to move and talk. Give me a thumbs up if you're ready to help Pedro do this.

"Okay, so page 1. Pedro is lying on the alligator pillow, with his brother, watching *The Magic School Bus*, right?

"Please use your white board and sketch that. And guys, are you going to sketch Pedro standing there with his hands at his side, watching TV? No! Pedro, will you show us how you were lying on that pillow so we can make the picture more exact?" Pedro threw himself across an imaginary pillow, chin propped in his hands, legs splayed.

"Writers, let's capture that on our white boards, making sure that we have no frozen characters." After children sketched, I said, "Now, writers, do you think the words should go:

Pedro watched TV.

"No? You think there are ways to write the words so the characters come to life? What words might unfreeze Pedro so that he comes to life on the page? Touch your white board and tell your partner what you think the story should say so that Pedro comes to life."

As the children talked, I called out a few tips.

"Remember to tell your story bit by bit. What happened next? His brother changed the channel, right? Picture that, everyone. What do you think that looks like? What do you think Pedro did when that happened? Might he have said something? Unfreeze those characters using your pictures and your words."

After a minute, I reconvened the group.

"Listen to this, everyone. Henry said, 'Pedro *flopped* onto his alligator to watch TV.' *Flopped*. What a great word! That's just what Pedro showed us he did, isn't it? I can see him flopping on his pillow. And after his brother changed the channel, Jordan and Lexie came up with this line: 'Pedro shouted, "No fair!"' And look," I held up their white board, "they drew Pedro trying to grab the remote out of his brother's hand.

"You're getting it. I can see the story coming to life. Isn't it like we are all in the room with Pedro and his brother, watching the story unfold?"

Then I said, "Right now, take out your story. I know you haven't finished it, but I want you to go back to the start of the story and touch and tell the pages, and then sketch page 1 again, this time adding in more details. And when you have sketched page 1, start writing that page. Plan on writing a whole bunch of sentences, not just one. Get started now, while I admire your work. Writers, thank you for helping Pedro bring his story to life. As you go back to sketch and write your story, remember what we did to tell Pedro's story bit by bit, and do that same work on your own."

Capturing Stories and Telling Them across Our Fingers

Engage students in thinking about how to catch story ideas, saving them for later.

"Writers, yesterday Lina Lee handed me a story she'd just finished. But her paper slipped out of her hand and floated like a magic carpet, down, down, and flew right inside the trash can. Lina Lee and I realized that what had just happened—her saying, 'I'm done!' and then dropping her story, and it floating down and landing in the trash—could make *another* story! She said, 'I could write a story about that.' And I told her, 'Catch that story idea, then.'

"I want to share with all of you a way writers catch story ideas. When Lina Lee realized, 'Wait, this could make a story!' she could catch the idea like this." I reached out as if I could catch Lina Lee's story in my hand and then shoved my hand, still holding the story, into my pocket. Pulling my hand out, I patted the pocket with pleasure. "Writers do that. They find stories everywhere in their lives, and they hold onto them," I said, again gesturing as if I were reaching for and holding onto a story, "until they can write them down."

Demonstrate taking a story out of your pocket (fist tight) and then telling your story by raising one finger for each part of the story and saying all you can that happened in that part before moving to the next finger.

"Then, later, you can always reach your hand into your pocket and take out a story. And you have a story helper, too, because you pull your story out like this."

I held my fist tight as if holding a story and held it up for the writers to see. "I have a story about one time when mud splashed all over me when I was going to the ice cream store." I raised my thumb, touched it and said, "One rainy day my mom and I were walking down the street." I started to raise my next finger and then put it down. I went back to my thumb and touched it to remind myself to say more about that first part of the story. "Wait, let me see if there is more to that part of the story. Hmm. Oh, we were going to the ice cream store. Okay, now I can go to the next part of the story." I touched my next finger. "What was the very next thing that happened? Oh right, all of a sudden a car drove by really fast and mud splashed all over me. What else can I say about that part? I know. I yelled, 'Oh no the mud is all over me!'" I held up my third finger. "Then my mom tried to help me get the mud off, but it was even in my hair! I said to my mom, 'Thank you.'" I held up my fourth finger. "What was the very next thing we did? I'm getting to the end of my story. I know. We decided to walk back home. And I said, 'I can't wait to get some clean clothes.'" I raised my last finger and said with a wrapping-up tone in my voice "I got home and changed into clean clothes. I said to my mom, 'I'm ready to go now!' And we went back out to the store." Did you see how I told one part of my story on each finger and I said as much as I could about what I did and said before going to the next finger to tell the next part? Now I'll be ready to write this story. When it is time to write, I can get a booklet and touch and tell it across pages and start sketching. I might have to add a couple pages because my story has five parts to it!"

Tell children to think of what they are going to write about, and then ask them to tell their stories across their fingers to their partners.

"Now I want you to catch a small moment in your minds and in one of your hands. Think of what you are writing about." I paused to give children thinking time. "You got it?" I held my closed fist out again. Most of the children copied me. "Now turn to your partner, and tell your moment using your fingers. Remember to say as much as you can about each part. Before you move to the next finger, think about what else you did or said in that part. Then when you are done with that part, think about the very next thing you did. When you only have two fingers left, you want to start finishing your story. Your story might only go across three fingers, or it might go across four or five like mine did."

The students turned to their partners and began to tell their stories using their fingers. As I listened in, I heard Katherine say, raising her thumb, "I went to the beach." She raised her second finger. "I went in the ocean." She paused, thinking about what else she could say about that. "I said, 'Dad come in the water!'" She raised her third finger. "Then we were splashing in the water. The waves crashed on us." Her fourth finger went up. "We got out of the water. My mom gave us our towels. She said, 'Dry off so we can go home.'" She stuck up her last finger and said, "Then we got in the car to go home."

Link the storytelling to the work students do when they sit down to plan a story.

Suggest to children that if they begin a new piece, it might help them to tell the story across their fingers first.

"You just told your moments across your fingers. Whenever you are writing a new piece, try planning the story across your fingers and see if this helps you tell it one step at a time, saying all you can on each finger and then thinking, 'What's the very next thing that happened?' as you move to the next finger."

It is important to find every imaginable way to bring home to children the central concepts you are trying to teach. This graphic organizer is a perfect way to help children develop an internalized sense of the shape of a story, and it will mean a lot to some children, especially to those who have difficulty when all our instructions rely on verbal communications.

The idea of telling a story across one's fingers came from Natalie Louis, and the truth is that lots of these minilessons rely on ideas that emerged only because a group of teachers and I were in a study group together. Remember that one of the best ways to invent beautiful teaching is to plan your teaching in the company of others!

Bringing What's Inside Out
Making Characters Think and Feel

IN THIS SESSION, you'll teach children that writers bring their stories to life by making characters think and feel.

GETTING READY

✔ Be prepared to sing "If You're Happy and You Know It" with students in the connection.

✔ A previous student's writing that exemplifies how writers show what they are thinking and feeling (see Teaching)

✔ Your shared class story from Session 8 (see Active Engagement)

✔ A mentor text or your own piece of writing to use when teaching children how to show, not tell, feelings in a conference or strategy groups

✔ "Ways to Bring Stories to Life" chart (see Link and Share)

✔ A ruler to use as a magic wand for the share, tapping writers to act out the strategies on the "Ways to Bring Stories to Life" chart

Y OU MAY BE WONDERING whether this day's teaching is within the reach of first-graders—whether they have the maturity and writing skills to weave emotion and thinking into their simple, sparse narratives. The answer is a resounding *yes*. If there's one thing young children live and breathe, it's emotion. They feel and express things in very pronounced ways: hysterics when they hear a silly joke, squeals of delight at the prospect of a trip or even just a play date or, on the flip side, fury at the destruction of their block creations, inconsolable sadness when told "no."

Children are natural storytellers, too; they arrive at school bursting at the seams with stories of how the dog ate the cold cuts off a platter meant for the family reunion, of how they learned a new card trick, of the new friend they made at the park and the hideout rock the two found that day. Nonetheless, chances are that many of these same children, when asked to put their stories onto the page, will end up writing pieces that feel more like lists of things they did than like the vibrant stories they tell in conversation. The challenge, then, is how to guide children to bring all of their passion and emotion to the page, to apply their knack for oral storytelling to their written work.

Today's teaching aims to help you channel this expressiveness into children's writing so that they identify and name the feelings of the people in their stories—and especially their own. For some children, it will be enough to write, simply, "I felt mad" or "I wanted that cake," while others will be able to add simple actions or gestures to their pictures—a foot stomping, a frown—that show the feelings and thinking of the people in their stories. Celebrate whatever your students produce—whatever they do to bring the inside out.

COMMON CORE STATE STANDARDS: W.1.3, W.2.3, W.1.5; RL.1.1, RL.1.3, RL.1.4; SL.1.1, SL.1.4; L.1.1, L.1.2, L.1.5.c,d

Bringing What's Inside Out

Making Characters Think and Feel

CONNECTION

Surprise your students by getting them to stand up and sing "If You're Happy and You Know It," using this song to spotlight that people show their feelings through actions.

"Writers, stand up!" I directed the kids with a conductor-like move. They looked surprised as they scooted off their bottoms and to their feet.

Without explanation, I began singing. "If you're happy and you know it, clap your hands, if you're happy and you know it, clap your hands, if you're happy and you know it and you really want to show it, if you're happy and you know it, clap your hands." The kids started clapping as I began a second round, this time gesturing for them to join in as we changed the lines from "clap your hands" to "stomp your feet."

After a few more rounds, I asked students to sit on the rug.

"Whew! How do you feel?" I asked.

The response was resounding, and chaotic. "Happy! Good! Tired!"

"You *look* happy," I said. "I see it on your faces and I felt it in your singing and in your clapping, and you know what? I can tell what you guys feel by listening to the things you say and watching what you do. That's really what that song is about: if you're happy and you know it and you really want to show it—do something!

"We could add a new verse." I sang, "If you're angry and you know it and you really want to show it . . . Do what?"

Children piped in with, "Kick the ground." "Yell at someone."

❧ **Name the teaching point.**

"Today I want to teach you that one way writers bring their stories to life is by including what their characters feel," I touched my heart, "and think." I tapped my head.

◆ COACHING

Whenever possible, think of ways to make a conection between something familiar to your writers and the new writing work that will be introduced today.

You might be surprised, but all of this has a lot to do with writing.

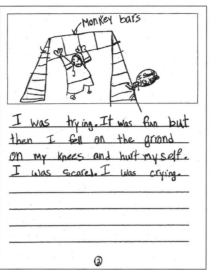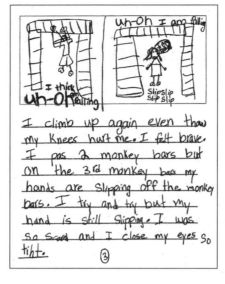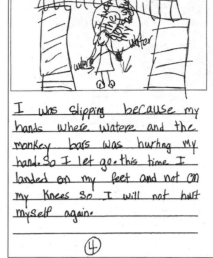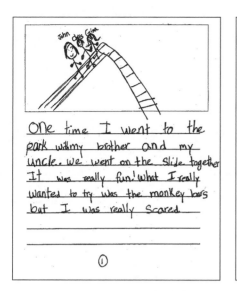

Panel 1:
One time I went to the park with my brother and my uncle. We went on the slide together. It was really fun! What I really wanted to try was the monkey bars but I was really scared.
①

Panel 2:
Monkey bars
I was trying. It was fun but then I fell on the ground on my knees and hurt myself. I was scared. I was crying.
②

Panel 3:
uh-oh I am falling
uh-oh I think falling
Slipslip slip slip
I climb up again even thau my knees hurt me. I felt brave. I pas a monkey bars but on the 3rd monkey bars my hands are slipping off the monkey bars. I try and try but my hand is still slipping. I was so scard and I close my eyes so tiht.
③

Panel 4:
water water
I was slipping because my hands where watere and the monkey bars was hurtng my hand. So I let go. this time I landed on my feet and not on my knees so I will not hurt myself again.
④

FIG. 10–1   Gina's story about climbing on the monkey bars in which she brings the inside out, revealing thoughts and feelings

Panel 5:
I hurt
I was kindof fun but I am still scared but I will try again." AHH.
⑤

TEACHING

Explain that teachers save student writing, especially instances in which writers' feelings are revealed. Then read aloud a saved piece, asking children to gesture when the feelings are revealed.

"Did you know that teachers collect the writing that kids do, often for years and years? It's true. Some people save things like their wedding dress or their babies' little booties. Teachers save children's writing. I have some pieces of writing that I've saved for years and years. The other day, I looked over some of those pieces, asking myself, 'Why are *these* the pieces that I saved?' And I realized that I saved many of these because there are places in them where there is a crack in the story (like a crack in an egg that holds a newborn chick), and you can see the writer's inside feelings.

"Let me read you one of those pieces of writing, and when you hear the part where Gina tells us her feelings, will you touch your heart? Then I'll read another part where she also *shows* us those feelings in a powerful way." (See Figure 10–1.)

Page 1: One time I went to the park with my brother and my uncle. We went on the slide together. It was really fun! What I really wanted to try was the monkey bars but I was really scared.

"I see so many of you touching your hearts. I bet you noticed that Gina told us how she was feeling. She said she was scared to try the monkey bars. That's one thing that writers do. They *tell* us how they were feeling, using feeling words. Now listen to the next page. Touch your heart when you hear the part where Gina really *shows* us her feelings."

Page 2: I was trying. It was fun but then I fell on the ground on my knees and hurt myself. I was scared. I was crying.

"I see lots of you have your hands on your hearts. What was Gina doing in the story to show us how she felt?" Kids began to pretend cry.

"Writers, I see so many of you pretending to cry. You look scared. She didn't just say she was scared, she also *showed* us she was scared by saying that she cried. I'll read another page. Let's look at the next page and look real closely at her sketch. She really brought the inside out in the sketch and in the words. This time listen for the parts when she tells us what she was *thinking*," I tapped my head, "and how she *felt*." I touched my heart. "Tap your head or touch your heart."

Page 3: Sketch: 'uh-oh I think I am falling' 'uh-oh I am falling' "I am falling" slip slip slip
       On the lines: I climb up again even though my knees hurt me. I felt brave. I passed 2 monkey
       bars but on the 3rd monkey bars my hands are slipping off the monkey bars. I try and try but my
       hand is still slipping. I was so scared and I closed my eyes so tight.

As I read, fingers tapped heads and hands touched hearts. "Turn and tell your partner all you noticed.

"Writers, many of you really liked how Gina wrote that she was thinking 'Uh-oh, I think I am falling' in the picture. We know she was feeling scared again. Then some of you said you noticed that she said how she closed her eyes really tight. She didn't just say she was scared, she showed us!"

ACTIVE ENGAGEMENT

Recruit the children to add feelings to the shared class story. Direct partnerships to turn and talk, saying what they were feeling during the story.

"Yesterday we realized that in our original fire drill story, we'd made ourselves seem like stick figures—as if we'd been frozen in a game of freeze tag—even though we were actually doing and thinking and feeling all kinds of things. If we want to let our readers know what we were thinking and feeling, we need to show those thoughts and feelings." I sang just the snippet, "If you really want to show it, clap your hands, stamp your feet, clench your fists—do something!

"Let's try adding thoughts and feelings. For me, I had some big thoughts and feelings when the alarm went off. Remember that: 'Clang, clang, clang went the bell.' Close your eyes and picture yourself here in our room when the bell went

In this teaching, a child's piece is used as a mentor text, and the strategies for revealing feelings and thoughts are discovered by studying the text closely. Remember that any text can be a mentor text—published books, teacher's pieces, class shared texts, and student pieces. It is important that writers see that we learn from a variety of authors, including the authors sitting right beside us!

off. What were you thinking? What were you feeling? Get that in your head. Now, open your eyes and tell your partner some lines you could add to show what was going on inside you," I tapped my head and my heart.

The room erupted into conversation. After a minute, I convened the writers. "Josh said, 'I was scared 'cause I thought the fire was gonna come in our room.' And listen to this. Marco said, 'I felt excited and I thought maybe we'd get to see a fire truck.' If you guys had written this fire drill story and added either of those parts, then you know what? I think I'd end up saving your writing for years and years!"

LINK

Remind writers that they now have many ways to make their characters come to life, adding today's new tip onto the chart.

"Writers, do you know what zombies are? They are pretend, spooky people," I said in a slow, lifeless voice, "who have no feelings or reactions to anything." I made my face blank and took a few weighted steps. "Are there any zombies in this room?" I looked from one kid to the next as the class giggled and shook their heads no. "No way, Jose! We weren't *zombies* when the fire drill happened, and we aren't zombies now! We could turn our fire drill story into a real heart-stopper if we put everything that was going on in our heads and hearts that day onto the page.

"Here's the thing. Listen up, 'cause this is important. Readers *always* want to know what characters are thinking and how they are feeling. They don't want to read about zombies any more than they want to read about frozen people. So today and any day you write, remember to make your people active. Tell us what they are doing, saying, thinking, and feeling. Bring your stories to life! Think you can do that?"

The kids nodded eagerly. "I am going to add that to our chart: Bring out what is inside—make people feel, make people think." (See Figure 10–2.)

> • Bring out the inside—make people feel, make people think

"Off you go then!"

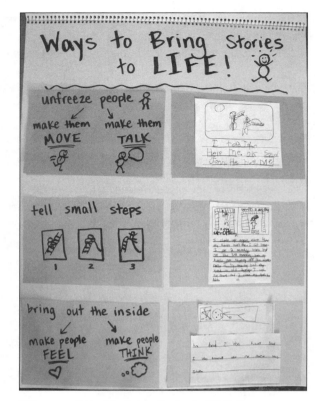

FIG. 10–2 "Ways to Bring Stories to Life" chart

The challenge when one is writing is to shift from retelling the chronological sequence of events to elaborating upon one event by describing how characters felt or thought at any one time. During conferences, I'll have to help children make the transition between the one and the other as they write.

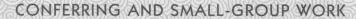

Inviting Students to Not Just Tell, but to *Show* Their Characters' Feelings

YOUR GOAL FOR YOUR FIRST-GRADE WRITERS is for them to begin telling the "inside" story of the characters, and that often looks like simple feeling statements across the story. This is good work—work you'll want most of your writers, if not all, to take on. At first some will be showing feelings by drawing facial expressions on the people in each scene. Today's session helps them really think about using words to tell and *then* try to use words to *show*, those feelings. You will want to notice which writers already use simple feeling statements. These writers are ready to show feelings in their stories, not just tell about them. Below

is a transcript of a writing conference I had to support one student with this work using a mentor text.

I sat down next to Skylah, who I could see was rereading one of her stories, flipping from page to page, and seemed unsure of what to do next. She had her pictures sketched and had written across the pages. (See Figure 10–3.) I asked, "Skylah, what are you working on in your writing today?"

"I'm trying to write like George McClements did," she responded.

(continues)

MID-WORKSHOP TEACHING Balancing Making Characters Move and Talk with Making Them Think and Feel

"Writers, can I stop you for a moment? I see so many of you have made the people in your story think and feel. Great work helping the reader see what is happening on the inside—in your heart and in your mind! Writers do this across the pages of their book, not just one time. One way to plan your stories is to use our storytelling tools—your fingers—to think about telling what the people in your stories did and said *and* telling what they felt and thought, *inside* their hearts and minds.

Here is the trick to doing that. When writers story-tell, they touch their fingers and say all they can in that part—action and talking. When they want to tell what happened on the inside, they slide their finger down in between their storytelling fingers and say what people thought or felt. Watch how I do that." I touched my

first finger. "One day I took my dog for a walk." I slid my finger between my fingers. "Hmm. What did I feel or think? Well, I was feeling happy because I hadn't seen my dog all day. Writers, did you see how I did that? I told the first part—saying *what I did*—and touched my first finger. Then, instead of going to the next finger, I slid my finger in between my two fingers to remind me to say what was happening on the inside, *what I felt or thought*.

"Writers, are you ready to give it a try? You can try it with the story you are working on now, or if you finished one, you could try it on a story you are going to write next. Get your story in your hands and hold up your fists when you have it." I waited for writers to catch those stories. "Okay, so try it with your partner. Partner 2, start. Tell your story, and then Partner 1, ask

questions. Make sure you ask your partner questions to get to know what the people were feeling or thinking." I listened as partners told their stories. Brendan touched each finger as he told his story. I whispered into Jazmin's ear, suggesting she ask him how he was feeling. She did, and Brendan giggled and said, "Oh right. I forgot!"

"Writers, you know how to tell stories that really come to life. You make people talk and move," I touched the top of my finger, "*and* think and feel." I touched the inside of my fingers. "Remember that before you write a story you can do this, and that will help you remember to put those important details in the story when you are writing your words."

  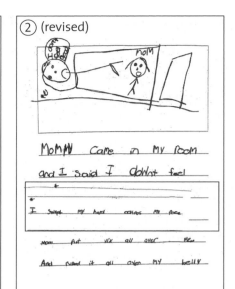 

Page 1: One day I was too sick to go to school. I had a bad cold so I stayed in bed. I was feeling sad. I was frowning and my nose was stuffy. (ADDED DURING CONFERENCE)

Page 2: Mommy came in my room and I said, "I don't feel good." Flap: (ADDED DURING CONFERENCE) I swept my hand across my face. "Okay you will stay home from school. Mom put vix all over me and rubbed it all over my belly.

Page 3: I heard my mom knocking on my door. "Can I get some soup?" I heard her knock on my door again. I shouted, "Put some chicken in my soup NOW!" I felt better.

FIG. 10-3 Skylah's story about being sick and staying home in bed in which she uses a mentor text to help her revise her story so that she shows, not tells, how she was feeling

"How are you trying to write like George McClements?" I asked.

"I want to say things like he did—squirming his body and twisting his toes because he didn't like that pea!"

"Oh," I said, "you are trying to show how you were feeling like George did?" She nodded. "Well, I can see how you already *told* us how you were feeling." I found the part where she told her feelings on the first page. "And have you tried, like George, to *show* that feeling anywhere in the story?" She pointed to the frown on her face in the sketch. "Well George did do that in his pictures, too. So you want to do it in the words, too?" She nodded again.

At this point, I reflected on what I knew about Skylah from my previous conferences, from this piece, and from conversation about her intentions. I knew she consistently

wrote small moments, focusing on single meaningful, ordinary events. She moved through the writing process independently. As I looked at the narrative learning progression on my clipboard, I glanced at the elaboration section, and she seemed to be working at the second-grade level. She consistently used action and dialogue, attempting to tell the story in step-by-step fashion. She recently had begun incorporating more of the inside story with feelings and thoughts and was ready to strengthen elaboration in that area. She wanted to use a mentor text to help her write better, and while "show, not tell" is a more advanced skill, I decided to go with that. This meant that I would continue to support her with her use of mentor texts, a lifelong skill for her as a writer.

I complimented the work she was already doing well as a writer, work I will build on when I teach her to do more sophisticated elaboration work. "You've done some great work already, Skylah! You are the kind of writer who knows how important it is to tell the reader what is happening on the inside, not just the outside. You wrote how you felt—that you were sad. You also are the kind of writer who knows that we learn from other authors. You knew you wanted to show feelings like George in *Night of the Veggie Monster*. I think you are definitely ready to be the kind of writer who tries the work from a mentor text, and in this case, tries a strategy that will help you begin to show, not just tell, how you were feeling in your stories. I'll help you with that, and then you will know how to do it anytime you are writing." She smiled up at me, showing me that she was ready to give it a try.

I put *Night of the Veggie Monster* in front of her on the table. I did a quick demonstration. "Let's see what George did to show how the little boy was feeling." I opened up to the page where his eyes were watering. "Well, on this page he told us about what happened to his eyes, right?" Then I turned the page and said, "On this page he told what happened to his toes. He's telling what his face and body did. Writers do that to show how the people in their stories are feeling.

"You can do that, too. Think back to a part where you had a strong feeling. It might be a part where you already *told* the reader how you felt. You can tell how you felt *and then show* how you felt by writing what your face and body were doing."

"When I was lying in my bed, I already said I was sad."

"Think what happened when you were lying in your bed feeling sad. What did you do? Think about your face and your body."

"I was in the bed. I said, 'I don't feel good,' but I already wrote that. I had a frown on my face. Oh! I could write that I had a stuffy nose. That was what was happening on my face."

"Oooh! That shows you were sad and feeling sick. Quick! Add it before you forget!"

"Skylah, you've discovered that when writers want to help readers feel something they were feeling in their stories, they often write what their faces and bodies were doing when they were feeling that way—like George does and like you are doing! Remember, you can do this often in this story and all of your writing."

Writers Have Lots of Ways to Bring Stories to Life

Teach children a game (unfreezing the statues) to help them review the list of strategies they have learned.

"Writers, let's play a game. Pretend you are statues. I'll be the magician. When I tap you with my wand," I waved a ruler in the air, "you will come to life, but only after you name one way you've learned to bring your stories to life. Once you've said something that helps bring your stories to life, I'll give you a signal to come to life. Then you can show us what that way looks like. Then I'll tap the next person."

I tapped the first child who called out, "Tell it in itsy-bitsy spider steps?" I gave her a thumbs up and she shook out her arms and legs and then took tiny steps across the carpet. I pointed to where it read "tell small steps" on the class chart. We continued until we had gone over all three strategies on the chart.

Ways to Bring Stories to Life

- "Unfreeze" people—make them move, make them talk
- Tell small steps
- Bring out the inside—make people feel, make people think

"What a list, writers! I bet maybe, just maybe, some of you might come up with your very own strategies for bringing your stories to life. If you do, I'll add it to our chart!"

Session 11

Using Drama to Bring Stories to Life

𝔇ear Teachers,

It has been our experience, over years of writing these Units of Study books, that it helps now and then to insert an overview of how a session might go—rather than a fully fleshed out write-up. These letters of suggestion allow you, the teacher, to take yet more ownership of this curriculum. Obviously, we assume (and hope!) you will tweak all these sessions to fit the needs of your particular class and your own teaching goals, but we also know that even the best of intentions fall away when a person is faced with so many pressing requests, tasks, expectations all at once—as every teacher we know always is! Therefore, we imagine many of you may be teaching the minilessons in this book largely as they are written. Having a few lessons that you then tailor to precisely fit the needs of your class of students and to also reflect your own interests gives you the opportunity to make this curriculum your own. Meanwhile, this gives you the opportunity to be creative and to self-assess—much as you'll ask students to do now and then, across a unit. This particular day is full of possibilities for fun, so we hope you'll enjoy designing the various parts. Here are some suggestions for how this day might go.

Today we invite you to capitalize on children's tendency to add drama and imagination to their play by incorporating a bit of acting into today's session. Watch children at play and you'll find that pretend play is very much like the writing process. Children come up with (and rethink) ideas and plans for stories that their dolls and action figures play out, bit by bit. They invent characters and settings and elaborate plots. If you listen closely, you will find that their play is laden with dialogue and actions, and it is this imaginary conversation between characters and the accompanying movement that makes their play come to life. Two children are in the block center, playing with a wooden knight and horse: "Watch out!" "We must save her!" "Oh no! Here comes a dragon!" "Aaargh!" And the quest or battle or ransacking begins. Another child is playing by herself on the playground: "Where did my pony go? Oh, there she is! Neigh! Neigh!" And off the child gallops into the sunset on her imaginary pony.

COMMON CORE STATE STANDARDS: W.1.3, W.1.5; RL.1.3; SL.1.1, SL.1.4; L.1.1, L.1.2

By having children do a bit of acting in today's lesson, children will be having fun, and meanwhile, you'll be setting them up to do some significant revision.

MINILESSON

In your connection you might read a few examples of students' stories that work particularly well, ones that include a lot of lively dialogue or small, precise actions or thinking and feeling, if any of your kids have included internal story.

Then you might hand over the reins to kids, talking up their growing independence. Perhaps you'll word the teaching point like this: "Writers, you are ready to take charge of your writing! Today I want to teach you that one way to bring a story to life is to act out what really happened, either with a partner or in your mind, noticing what you need to add."

During your demonstration, you might act out one of your own stories, using gestures and an animated voice to bring out the drama. Ask kids to follow along with you, lifting their arms or making a scared face or putting their hands on their hips as you do. They'll love doing this with you and will also have a chance to see that a good story is one that can be acted out. As you demonstrate, you might pause at some point to say, "Wait a minute. How did I respond? Oh yeah! I said . . . ," and then add that into the story, so that kids have a model of how to revise on the go during this bit of acting.

During the active engagement, have kids stand up in their rug spots and work with a partner to act out a part of their own stories. Remind them to notice and make a mark on the page when they think they could add something—a bit of dialogue or more action. Listen in as kids do this, coaching in to this work.

When you send children off to write, remind them that the work they did with their partner is work they can do on their own, too, now and any time they write. They can act out their writing sitting in their own seats, mentally or physically taking note of what they want to add. You can add this to the "Ways to Bring Stories to Life" chart. Remind them that chilren are the bosses of their writing and that they can decide on their own what needs fixing and which strategies they'll use to do the fixing.

CONFERRING AND SMALL-GROUP WORK

You can coach partners to hold their pen in their hand the entire time, even when acting out, so that they can make changes to their writing at any point. This way, partner time is more than simply taking turns reading to one another. It is a time for partners to help each other revise their writing.

With the focus so heavy on making stories come to life (which is really a kid-friendly way of saying writing with detail and voice), it's possible that some of your students might need friendly reminders to use some of the mechanics of writing they know well, especially now that so many children are attempting to add more dialogue. While you don't want the mechanics to become the main focus of your work, you may find it is helpful to do quick reminder lessons about spacing, capitalization, and using the word wall.

You could take the first few minutes of writing time to stand back and do some informal assessment by circulating around the room and jotting down some lists of students who need a quick reminder. Tap three or four students on the shoulder and quietly pull them aside for a brief strategy lesson. A simple quick reminder and a few minutes of guided practice will help them keep mechanics on their radar, without consuming all their energy for writing.

If you notice mechanical problems in students' writing that will take more than a quick reminder, make some notes to yourself that these might be good groups to pull near the end of this bend or later on in the unit when editing is a main focus. As much as you might want to introduce brand new work for mechanics and grammar, working on heavy duty, new mechanics and conventions right now might distract kids from the main goal in this bend—writing with detail and voice, making their stories come to life for the reader. Save the important work of introducing new or challenging strategies for mechanics for when the time is right.

In individual conferences today, don't forget to help students bring their writing to life. Acting parts out is just one of many strategies that may help lift the level of your students' writing.

MID-WORKSHOP TEACHING

During your mid-workshop teaching, you might emphasize that this kind of acting can help even when writers are only one page into a story. Specifically, when kids act out even the beginning of a piece, it can help them see what kind of details they need to add and whether they are tending to overly depend on one way of writing at the expense of another. Some kids write lots of actions but forget to include talking or thinking, while others write pieces that are heavily laden with talking, but whose characters effectively talk while standing still. Acting out their writing will help children see what kind of writer they are and what they need to add to their work to show more action.

SHARE

During the teaching share, you might refer to the questions that help writers revise on the process chart ("How to Write a Story") from Session 3 to remind them of questions partners can ask to help each other revise: Who? Where? When? What? How?

Good Luck!

Lucy, Abby, and Rachel

Using Familiar Words to Spell New Words

IN THIS SESSION, you'll teach children that writers use words they know to spell new and more challenging words.

GETTING READY

✔ A story by a student who needs help spelling one or more words similar to those on the word wall (see Teaching)

✔ White boards and markers, to be used during the active engagement, mid-workshop teaching, and share

✔ Magnetic letters for students to manipulate words during conferring

✔ "Ways to Spell Words" chart from Session 4, to add to during the Link and Mid-Workshop Teaching

✔ "Ways to Bring Stories to Life" chart to review during the Link

TODAY'S SESSION BUILDS UPON your children's growing command of sight words, words found on your classroom walls, and familiar words from word study. You've probably been studying high-frequency words such as *went* and *look* during word study, shared reading, and interactive writing, and words such as these are probably featured on your word wall. You might also have words that highlight the features you are studying in word study on the word wall or on a separate spelling pattern chart. For example, you might have *can* and *bat* in the room for children to use to spell other words with the same rimes. Your students probably write with the knowledge that there are words like these that they don't sound out—words they either just know or can find on the word wall or in the room. Today's session helps children understand that words they know are tools for spelling new words. Just as you've begun nudging your children to read unfamiliar words by drawing on ones they know, you will now help them use words they already know (including high-frequency words and words around the classroom) to help them spell words they don't already know how to spell.

This attention to spelling may seem to you to interrupt work you've been doing on writing fluent and detailed stories, but actually, spelling is essential precisely because children want to write lively narratives. To write with dialogue, detail, and action, children need to write with more resourcefulness, making it important for them to be active problem solvers as they write. That problem solving will need to include spelling.

By helping children draw on the words they already know how to spell to tackle words they want to write, you help them progress from spelling in a phoneme-by-phoneme way toward hearing and recording chunks of words. The work in this session requires children to be able to hear parts of words that are the same to write unfamiliar words more efficiently. You will also want to support this important work during your word study time.

COMMON CORE STATE STANDARDS: W.1.3; RFS.1.2, RFS.1.3; SL.1.1; L.1.1, L.1.2.d,e

Using Familiar Words to Spell New Words

CONNECTION

Using an example from class, point out that children can use words they already know to help them spell words they don't yet know.

"Writers, I want to tell you something really exciting. Yesterday I saw Jesse look at the word wall and copy down a word, but when I checked to see which word he had copied, I didn't see any of our word wall words. So I said, 'Jesse, I saw you copying something from the word wall, but I don't see any words from the word wall in your story!'

"Then Jesse said, 'It's right here!' and pointed to the word *ran* in his story. 'I *ran* down the hill.' That confused me because *ran* wasn't listed under the *r* on our word wall. 'Yeah,' Jesse said, '*Ran* is just like *can* on our word wall.' When Jesse said that, writers, I realized that he wasn't using the word wall just to copy a word. He was using the word wall to figure out how to spell a new word!"

❖ **Name the teaching point.**

"Writers, today I want to teach you that when you want to write a word you don't know how to spell, it helps to find a word you already know that sounds like it, like Jesse did. Once you find a word you know with a part that sounds the same as the word you want to spell, you can write that part! Then you only have to figure out the new part of your hard word!"

It can be especially powerful to use students in your class as an example, not only for the connection, but also when demonstrating a teaching point about spelling words. Many first-graders need a great deal of encouragement to take risks when it comes to problem solving words, often looking to you for help with spelling. Therefore, highlighting writers who've done this work, as Jesse has done in this classroom, or writers who are interested in using strategies for writing words, as Sabrina is in this teaching, motivates other writers to work independently and try their best.

TEACHING

Using an example from one child's story, show the class how to problem solve an unknown word by making connections to a word they already know.

"Now I'll show you how to try this. Sabrina is working on her story about how she took a box of cereal out of the cabinet and knocked it over by accident, spilling the Cheerios everywhere. Yesterday she wanted to write the word *took*, but she didn't know how to spell it. Let's help Sabrina write *took* now. Let's say the word *took* into our hands," I cupped my hands and held them near my mouth, "and listen to how it sounds, and then think, 'Does this word sound like another word I know? Does it sound like a word on our word wall?'"

To problem solve the spelling of a word with the class, select words from a child's story that will work best for your children and their knowledge of words. If the words from this lesson's story seem too complex for your writers, choose simpler words now and use more sophisticated words in future spelling lessons.

The children said the word into their cupped hands. "Remember, listen to how it sounds. Listen to the parts." I pointed to the word wall to remind them to be looking and trying out words. Children's eyes scanned the word wall as they read words from it, contrasting them with *took*. I heard, "Took, the." One child shook his head and looked back at the wall to try another word. Another child repeated, "Took, look. Took, look," and popped his thumb up. More thumbs popped up as other students found *look*.

"Yes, *took* and *look* rhyme. The parts at the end sound the same. I'll write 'look' on the side of my paper. Hmm, but I know *took* doesn't start with the /l/ sound! I will cross that part out. I know *took* starts with a *t*, so I'll write that! Here's my word now: 'took!'

"Did you see how we did that? Writers, when you get to a word you don't know that isn't on the word wall, you don't always need to stretch the word out, sound by sound. Instead, you can check to see if the word *sounds like* a word on the word wall or a word you know. You can write down the part that is the same. Afterward, you can write the rest of the letters. Just think, writers, how much faster you can spell words this way!" (See also Figure 12–1.)

When you have tools in your classroom like a word wall, it is important to actually teach children how to use these. Act out how you go about finding a word on the word wall. Show children that if you want to write school *and it is on the word wall, you don't copy the word letter for letter. Instead, you look at it, noticing whatever stands out.* School *sounds like it should contain a* k *but instead it begins with* sch. School *contains two* o's. *Once a child has noticed surprising features in a word, the child should be able to write the word without copying.*

The words you have posted on the word wall should be ones that children use often in their writing, or words they would like to use.

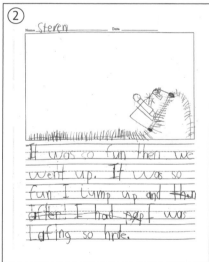

Page 1: I went on the small roller coaster. I was soo excited. I went on. It started to move. My dad screamed. It was so funny.

Page 2: It was so fun. Then we went up. It was so fun. I jump up and I was laughing so hard.

Page 3: After I had popcorn and then I went home. I kind of want to go again.

FIG. 12–1 Steven's story about going on a roller coaster in which he problem solved the word *jump* by thinking of a word he already knew—*bump*

ACTIVE ENGAGEMENT

Set children up to spell another word using this strategy.

"Okay, can you help Sabrina with one more word, this time working on your own? She is working on *crunch* because when she bent over to pick up the cereal she spilled, she stepped on some of those Cheerios and heard *crunch*. We're going to use words in our room *and* words we already know to try to help Sabrina spell *crunch*. Let's try to write the word *crunch* on our white boards.

"It isn't a word most of us just know, but let's check to see if it sounds like any words we do know. Hmm. Crunch." I began to look around the room, showing that I was thinking about words in our room. "Say it into your hand. Crunch. Do you know a word that has the same part at the end?" "Lunch!" Children pointed to the daily schedule where they saw "lunch." "Yes! We have lunch on the schedule. We read it everyday. Write *lunch* on your white boards.

"Which part of *lunch* is the same as *crunch*? Say *crunch* again and listen to the part that is the same."

"Unch," kids chorused.

"So, which letter can we take away from *lunch*?" "*L*," children said as they erased the *l*.

"Now let's write the letters at the beginning of *crunch*. Say the part you hear at the beginning of the word." The children said /cr/ into their hands. "Tell your partner any words that can help us write that part."

The children chattered busily. "I know, it's like *cry* and *crayon*."

"Great thinking, writers! Many of you said *cry*, so I have written it on the board. Which letters from this word will help us write *crunch*? Once you know, write them on your board next to *unch*.

"Let's reread the whole word: *Crunch!* Great work, writers. You used two words to help you solve this one hard word!"

LINK

Debrief, emphasizing how this strategy can help writers add to their Small Moment stories.

"Writers, you've been working hard on your stories to make them come to life. I know you want to get your words down as fast as you can, so you don't forget all that you want to say on each page. You know you can write words really quickly when you already know them. You write them in a snap. Today I hope you have learned that you can write words *almost* that quickly when you don't know how to spell a word by thinking of a word that sounds like the hard word.

The truth is it is crucial for children's reading as well as for their writing that they develop a repertoire of words they know with automaticity. The easiest words will be nouns and pronouns such as Mom *and* me. *These words, and others that are a bit harder, can be displayed on the word wall. Teach children that if they want to write a word they almost know by heart and it's on the word wall, they should look at the wall, fix it into their mind, then try to write it from memory. That way children are constantly growing their repertoire of known words.*

"You say the word, match it with a word you already know, then write down the part of the word that sounds the same, and then write the rest of the letters. Writers, I've added 'Use words you know' to our chart of ways to spell words." I reread the chart, now with the new strategy.

Ways to Spell Words

- Say it, slide it, hear it, write it
- Use snap words
- Listen for little words inside
- Use words you know

"You have so many ways to spell words, which means you can get even more words down on the page now during writing time. Remember that writers always work to write more on each page, telling the reader exactly what happened in each part of the story.

"As you start working today, you may want to reread your story and think carefully about all the words you will write on the page before you write them. And remember, too, that you will be trying to make your stories come to life." I pointed to and reread that chart and invited the students to read with me.

"Writers, are you ready to reread the stories you have been working on and then get started spelling words the best you can? Go ahead!"

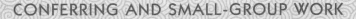
Supporting Writers in Working with Parts of Words, Rather than Just Letters

BEGINNING READERS AND WRITERS must learn to become flexible word solvers who use the words and spelling features they know to tackle unfamiliar language. This involves students making connections between words, often identifying a rhyming word and then adding, deleting, or substituting letters to make the new word. Since this work can be challenging, in your conferring, you might pull together small groups of writers who need support in building and manipulating words.

Plan to use conferring time to do some of the work with magnetic letters that you are probably doing in word study. Magnetic letters allow students to see, in a concrete way, connections between words and to see the process of changing parts of words to make new words.

(continues)

MID-WORKSHOP TEACHING   **Writing Part by Part, not Letter by Letter**

"Writers, you are brave spellers, spelling even tricky words the best you can! You are using words you know to find parts of words you are trying to write. That's a great strategy! I want to remind you that you also know spelling patterns from word study. You know letters that go together to make sounds like /at/, /ap/, and /sh/ and /st/. Now that you know those, you don't have to write letter by letter! You can write part by part!" (See Figure 12–2.)

"Writing part by part, let's help Spencer with a tricky word he is writing: *standing*. First, let's say the word. *Standing*. Now let's say the first part. Listen for sounds that go together that make a part we know. /St/. You know that blend: we've found it in our books when we read. Now write it on your white board, just like that." I wrote it on my own white board. "What's the next part? Reread and say the next part. What is it? Yes, /and/. Do we know it?"

"It's a snap word," announced a few children as others pointed to the word wall.

"Yes, we know *and* from the word wall. Write it quickly." I wrote *and* next to *st* on my white board. "Reread and say the next part. What is it? Yes, /ing/. Do we know it?"

"It's like *sing*."

"Like *king*!"

"Write /ing/ because that is the part that is the same. I'll write it on my board. You write it on yours. Now, writers, let's reread the word part by part. Slide your finger under each part, saying the sound that part makes. Does it look right?" I agreed with the chorus of yeses. "Writers, I'm adding 'part by part' to our chart of ways to spell words."

> • Write it part by part

"Go back to your stories and reread what you've written on the page to see which word you are going to write next. Thumbs up when you know the word. Say the word into your hand. Now say the first part. Say the rest of the parts. Now write that word, part by part!"

(continues)

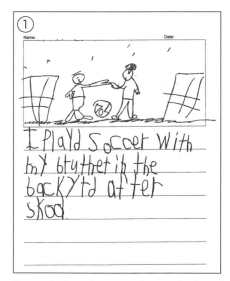
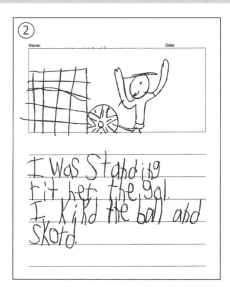
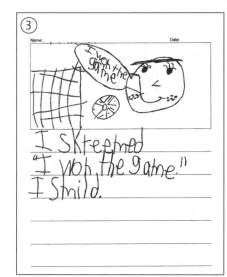

Page 1: I played soccer with my brother in the backyard after school.

Page 2: I was standing right near the goal. I kicked the ball and scored.

Page 3: I screamed "I won the game." I smiled.

FIG. 12–2 Spencer's soccer goal story where he wrote the word *standing* part by part

Children might need to begin by first practicing hearing patterns of sound. If they've been studying short vowel spelling patterns such as *at, ap,* or *an,* you might say a word like *fan* and ask students to think of a word they know that has a part that sounds the same at the end. Once they say a word that rhymes, like *can,* ask them to make that known word with the magnetic letters and then change the *c* to *f.* Once they are able to do this work with simple CVC (consonant/vowel/consonant) words that they've encountered in word study, have them try with high-frequency words they've been learning. You may want to consider using simpler words like those in the minilesson if your class is still learning some of the more basic sight words and is just beginning work with hearing and manipulating parts of words. When doing this practice during writing workshop, remember to give students time to try this work on words from their own stories. That will support them in learning to use this strategy independently.

At this point in the unit you will want to be checking to see that students are transferring the knowledge they are gaining about word solving to their writing. Since your word study has shifted from reviewing letter sounds to noticing spelling patterns, you will want to make sure that writers are figuring out how to spell words using these patterns. One way to teach this is to show them how to spell words by moving through them part by part. For example, if a child is spelling *stop,* then he should be thinking about problem solving the word one part at a time rather than walking through the word, ponderously, sound by sound. Rather than saying "s-t-o-p," the child should be able to hear *st* and *op* and write those quickly and accurately. Today's mid-workshop teaching will support this work, but some children will need extra support with using the spelling features from word study to do this problem solving. It can be helpful to have them bring word study charts or a word study notebook—any tool to remind them of the spelling features they've been learning—to writing workshop. Even if students can read and write words in isolation during word study using these spelling features, they may need explicit instruction and coaching to transfer that knowledge to their own writing. You may use prompts such as "Say the first part. Do you know that part? Write it."

As your writers become more courageous spellers, they will feel more confident working through multisyllabic words. Your strongest spellers will be representing most sounds in these complex words with letters and using what they know about words as they problem solve. Even these spellers, you will notice, sometimes leave off letters, especially letters in the middle or end. For example, even a strong speller might write *butterfly* as *buterf* or *buterfy*, missing sounds that in one-syllable words they don't usually leave out. It can be helpful to teach these spellers to problem solve words one syllable at a time to make sure they include all the letters for each syllable. Children probably come from kindergarten knowing how to clap syllables in words, so this is an important time to connect that phonological awareness work to spelling words. If a word has three syllables, they may need to problem solve each syllable in a different way. For example, one syllable may be a known word, another may have a part from another word, and one syllable may need to be stretched out sound by sound. You can coach writers to clap the syllables and then start with the first syllable and ask, "How will I spell this part?" Then move to the next syllable and do the same.

Word Solving Independently

Ask children to solve a word on their own and then share their method with others at their table. Highlight all the ways they've learned to tackle hard words.

"Writers, I saw you using so many different ways to figure out how to spell new words today! And I think this is so cool because I know this means you are doing something that professional writers always do. You are solving your own problems. Let's celebrate how great you've become at this work by doing some word solving together. Take up your white board.

"Let's say you were writing a story about how you came into the kitchen for dinner, and you were running so fast that you bumped the table and all the drinks spilled on the table. You wanted to write *spilled*. How would you go about word solving *spilled*? Work on your white board.

"Thumbs up when you finish writing the word. Now turn and talk to other writers at your table. How many ways did people at your table use to figure out this word? Share the methods you used to problem solve *spilled*." Children talked.

After a bit, I interrupted to say, "Writers, walking among you, I heard lots of different strategies for writing *spilled*. I heard that you stretched out the sounds of the word, then slid your finger along the board, and you wrote the word. I heard you used the word wall. You said the word *will* to figure out how to write *spilled*. These two words have a part that sounds alike: *-ill*. Great work, writers! You've all showed me that you can use lots of different strategies for figuring out how to write new words. And remember, anytime you come to a tricky word, you can rely on either of these strategies, or any other strategy you've learned, to spell the word, even if it's a word you've never spelled before."

You'll want to do this sort of work at other times in the day as well as now. Children need to be taught to use the tools and strategies of a writing workshop. Don't assume anything!

Editing
Capital Letters and End Marks Help Readers

ear Teachers,

You've reached the end of another bend in this unit!

In the first bend of the unit, you helped students understand the fundamentals of getting their stories down on paper independently. In essence, you helped them learn how to get ideas, how to focus, how to rehearse what they would say across pages, how to work with partners, and how to stretch out words so they could get down more writing for their readers.

Then, in this second bend, you worked through the process with your little writers again, this time suggesting they push themselves just a bit more. With each session, you offered up not just a way to be a writer, but a way to improve the quality of writing. You offered up to these first-graders ways to bring their stories to life, ways to unfold a plot, and ways to put even more words on paper, fluently. Now, before bringing children yet another set of ways to bring strength and depth to their writing, as you'll do in the next bend, here is one last session. What is the most helpful strategy you can teach these children today?

At this point in the unit, young writers tend to be perfectly ripe to learn to use a few more conventions, like punctuation, to help their readers. Their growing awareness of audience, as they ready themselves for the second mini-celebration, gives them energy to use what they know to make their readers more engaged with their stories. Today, then, you might teach children ways to use punctuation to help readers get more out of their stories. Then, in the share, you can prepare a bulletin board display case of writing for a hallway audience to appreciate and respond to. Here is one way today's session might go.

MINILESSON

In the connection today, instead of reminding children of all they know about conventions that could apply to their writing now, as you usually would, you could instead simply motivate them to work hard to edit for their readers.

COMMON CORE STATE STANDARDS: W.1.3; RFS.1.4.a,b; SL.1.1; L.1.1.j, L.1.2.b

You could use a small story from your life, about someone reading your writing, to explain why conventions matter. "Writers," you might say, "The other day, I left my writing on my kitchen table at home. This is what I had written so far." Then, you would read a tiny story like this one, slowly, to let the story sink in, and you'd use intonation and dramatic pauses.

I let my bunny hop around my living room. I went to get a glass of water, and when I got back
. . . he was chewing on the lamp cord! I yelled "No! No! No! Flurry!" and grabbed him away from
there as fast as I could.
When I hugged him, my hands were trembling because the lamp almost fell on him.

You could continue, "My husband came by and he loves stories, so he picked it up. And this is how he read it." At this point, you would read the same story monotonously and without pause or any inflection, even at the end of the implied sentences, leaving us feeling flat and even confused.

I-let-my-bunny-hop-around-my-living-room-I-went-to-get-a-glass-
of-water-and-when-I-got-back-he-was-chewing-on-the-lamp-cord-
I-yelled-no-no-no-Flurry-and-grabbed-him-away-from-there-as-fast
as-I-could-when-I-hugged-him-my-hands-were-trembling-because-the-lamp-almost-fell-on-him.

"Isn't that terrible? It is such an important story, and he read it just like that, like blah blah blah. I was so mad! I told him that didn't even sound like my story. 'There's nothing in the story at all, the way you read that!' I said to him. And he told me, 'Well, that's the way you wrote it. Look.' And he held it up for me to see, and you know, he was right. I had no marks to show him how to read it! Look, here it is."

At this point, you could unveil the story, written out on chart paper with no punctuation. Then you could ask children to read the first part of this story to their partner and decide what they could do to the page—what marks they could add to help my husband, or any reader, read it better next time.

After they've talked with their partners for a moment and you've collected some suggestions, you could name the teaching point. You could say, "Writers use marks on the page to help their readers read their stories in ways that make them great stories. Writers use lots of marks to do that: exclamation points for very important stops and periods for calm stops, for example. Writers also use capital letters when they are starting a new part." Of course, you could say even more, perhaps explaining that writers add commas for small breaks. You can also save that sort of thing to tuck into your demonstration, but not explain it in your teaching point. (This is a way of differentiating your instruction—offering up a bit more teaching for those children who are ready to take in more.)

For the teaching part of this minilesson, you can decide how much demonstration children need and demonstrate by thinking aloud as you punctuate your piece of writing. Be sure to consider putting punctuation in some wrong places, then reading it abiding by the punctuation, and deciding it doesn't go there. Be sure to also put periods where exclamation points should go, and vice versa, to help students feel what it is like to make a punctuation decision. This kind of deliberate "messing up" is important to model for students so you can catch yourself and then go back and revise. You will not need to punctuate the whole piece as a demonstration. You can see how much practice your particular students need. As you finish demonstrating, be sure to go back and check aloud for capital letters at the starts of your thoughts. That particular convention is hard to "hear," so we have to teach it as a habit, as something writers always check for as they get their writing ready for readers.

For the active engagement portion of the minilesson, ask children to finish punctuating this piece with their partners, testing out their decisions along the way by rereading it. As they work, gather some of their decisions and put them on chart paper. After they've done a bit of work, call for their attention and read the punctuated piece. If possible, invite a teacher or older student from the next-door class to read the short piece aloud, to test if the added punctuation helps the reader read it correctly. (This might take a little prep ahead of time, to be sure the reader knows to read with especially dramatic intonation.)

Sum up the minilesson for children by reminding them that writers always use punctuation and conventions to help their readers. Let them know that at the end of writing time today you will be setting up a display of their writing and that they each need to select one piece of writing and use punctuation as best they can to help readers get the most out of the story. And let them know that in this same way, whenever a story is going out to readers, writers always need to check their conventions.

CONFERRING AND SMALL-GROUP WORK

Some of your conferring time today will be helping children learn to assess their own writing and make a new goal based on the Narrative Writing Checklist you've posted or handed out and that they reviewed in Session 7. Remember to help those children by teaching them *how* to self-assess, coaching them in ways to look for a quality or feature in their writing. You might do this by demonstrating with a small sample of your own writing, using the same checklist. We recommend that you fight the urge to give children a goal. Your aim will be to teach each child how to make a goal for herself, based carefully on her own writing. By offering the checklist to begin with, you know the goal will be within the realm of what is helpful to her. Imagine how much more invested she may be if she makes the goal herself, based on evidence she finds on her own.

Today, as in every day's conferring, you will be coaching children on a wide variety of topics, depending on their needs, strengths, and purposes. In addition to children needing some coaching in self-assessment, there are bound to be a few children who need support understanding how writers use punctuation. By now, in reading workshop, many of your children are reading level E and F books, and at those levels, some of your reading instruction will be about helping them attend to punctuation. (In books at these levels, you may recall, phrases and sentences tend to be separated by line breaks; new sentences start on new lines. Because of this, it is easy for readers to follow the cue of the line break for a pause, never noticing the nearly invisible periods.) Since they may not be automatically attending to punctuation in their reading, it is easy to see why children may have to listen extra carefully for where the punctuation should go in their writing. In their own writing, of course, the end of a sentence may not fall at the end of a line!

You might try conferring with a youngster or with a small group of youngsters, using a book they know well. You can read it aloud dramatically, stopping when there is a period, pointing to it as you do so.

You could say, "These periods are like red lights when I am driving. They say, 'Stop for a second; take a breath!' Let me show you." Then you could read, placing a finger under each word and, at a period, pause dramatically, taking an exaggerated breath and popping your finger onto the period. Then you could say, "You try it. Let the periods tell you when to stop." If needed, you could demonstrate how it feels to read writing with no end punctuation. Then you could help the writer or writers get started, listening for where periods should go and adding them. "Will you read your writing the way it is supposed to go?" You could ask. "Put your finger where you want your reader to stop for a bit. Now go back and add a period. You've got it. This is what writers *always* do."

Near the end of the workshop today, you will probably want to gather up the writing that children have selected and punctuated so that you can get ready to display it just as you did at the end of the first bend. You may want to do this bit by bit so that by the end of the workshop, just before the share, the display is ready. If children have more time after their writing is on display, they can simply keep writing, as always. At the end of workshop, students will celebrate the work they've done so far, quietly reading each other's stories and jotting brief feedback (for example a happy face at a favorite part) on sticky notes. Children can add their sticky note compliments to the display themselves, or you can help.

MID-WORKSHOP TEACHING

By this point in the unit, you've helped children remember all they've learned about writing narratives in kindergarten, and you've started raising the bar. Now children have learned a few more things that writers do and strive to do and they've even started transferring some of the second-grade goals into their writing—or reaching for these goals. It will help them use these strategies and try for these

Narrative Writing Checklist

	Grade 1	NOT YET	STARTING TO	YES!	Grade 2	NOT YET	STARTING TO	YES!
	Structure				**Structure**			
Overall	I wrote about when I did something.	☐	☐	☐	I wrote about *one time* when I did something.	☐	☐	☐
Lead	I tried to make a beginning for my story.	☐	☐	☐	I thought about how to write a good beginning and chose a way to start my story. I chose the action, talk, or setting that would make a good beginning.	☐	☐	☐
Transitions	I put my pages in order. I used words such as *and* and *then, so*.	☐	☐	☐	I told the story in order by using words such as *when, then,* and *after*.	☐	☐	☐
Ending	I found a way to end my story.	☐	☐	☐	I chose the action, talk, or feeling that would make a good ending.	☐	☐	☐
Organization	I wrote my story across three or more pages.	☐	☐	☐	I wrote a lot of lines on a page and wrote across a lot of pages.	☐	☐	☐
	Development				**Development**			
Elaboration	I put the picture from my mind onto the page. I had details in pictures and words.	☐	☐	☐	I tried to bring my characters to life with details, talk, and actions.	☐	☐	☐
Craft	I used labels and words to give details.	☐	☐	☐	I chose strong words that would help readers picture my story.	☐	☐	☐
	Language Conventions				**Language Conventions**			
Spelling	I used all I knew about words and chunks of words (*at, op, it*, etc.) to help me spell.	☐	☐	☐	To spell a word, I used what I knew about spelling patterns (*tion, er, ly*, etc.).	☐	☐	☐
	I spelled all the word wall words right and used the word wall to help me spell other words.	☐	☐	☐	I spelled all of the word wall words correctly and used the word wall to help me figure out how to spell other words.	☐	☐	☐

qualities of writing if you cycle back to them again and again, allowing for more practice each time. Halfway through the writing time today is a good time to remind children of all they know and have learned. Is it all in their writing? You could refer back to the Narrative Writing Checklist.

Invite children to use the checklist to look over their nearly finished or finished piece of writing, filling it out as they do so. Then they could use a sticky note to write themselves a compliment based on something they've done well according to the checklist. After giving them a moment to do that, you might ask them to write another compliment to themselves about something they've done well that is above and beyond the checklist's goals—perhaps taking a risk or writing about something no one else in the class has written about (a social risk) or writing more than they've ever written or trying something else that was hard to do. You might collect both compliments for each child and post them near children's final pieces on the bulletin board or display.

As you send children off to write, you can ask them to look over their self-assessment checklist one more time and set a goal for their next piece of writing, perhaps a second-grade goal, writing it on a sticky note and saving it in their folders so that they can stick that goal onto the new blank pages they use for their writing in the next bend.

One day I went to the park. I slide on the slide down. Then I saw a friend. Her name was Xenia.

Maybe Xenia could play with me. I asked Xenia, "Do you want to play with me?"

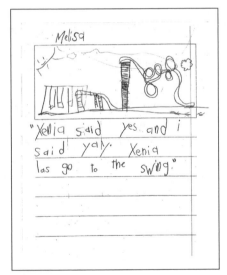

Xenia said, "Yes," and I said, "Yay." "Xenia let's go to the swing."

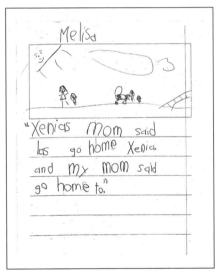

Xenia's mom said, "Let's go home Xenia." And my mom said, "Go home too."

FIG. 13–1   Melisa's story about playing with her friend at the park shows her work of making stories come to life with dialogue and a strengthening in her spelling skills as she's learned to rely on the word wall and problem-solving strategies.

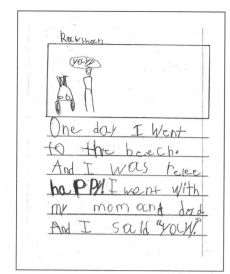   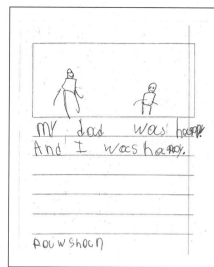

One day I went to the beach. And I was really happy! I went with my mom and dad. I said, "Yay."

I saw a boy running. The boy smashed my castle and I was sad.

And my dad helped. I said to my dad, you are the best!

My dad was happy. And I was happy.

FIG. 13–2 Rawshan's story about his dad helping him rebuild a sand castle shows how he is developing the skill of making characters come to life by using dialogue and feeling words throughout the story, including an ending that was added after the piece was completed.

SHARE

For these last ten or fifteen minutes of workshop time today, stand back together with your class and enjoy the writing children have created as a mini-celebration! At the very least, invite some children to read their own or a classmate's piece aloud for all to appreciate. If the writing is hard to decode, you or the author can be the reader, reading it as though it is the most brilliant piece of writing ever seen. It is certain to be easy to find a way to celebrate all the work children have done so far. The pride and enthusiasm you help them feel today will be transformed into new energy and resilience and stamina for the work of tomorrow.

Enjoy!

Lucy, Rachel, and Abby

Studying a Story to Learn Ways the Author Makes It Special

IN THIS SESSION, you'll teach children that writers study other authors' craft, seeing what special things the authors do that they could try in their own writing.

GETTING READY

✔ An enlarged version of a mentor text your class is familiar with that is chock-full of craft moves students will be able to spot and comment on, including ones they've tried themselves and new ones (we recommend *Night of The Veggie Monster*, but there are many other wonderful books you might use)

✔ Copies of the mentor text for each student (if possible)

✔ Small stickers (stars or smiley faces) for students to use to mark places in the text where they notice the author doing things that make the book special

✔ "Learning Craft Moves from a Mentor Author" chart with headings prewritten (see Teaching and Active Engagement). This chart will anchor your study of the text.

✔ A student's piece of writing to study the craft moves used (see Share)

COMMON CORE STATE STANDARDS: W.1.3, W.1.7; RL.1.1, RL.1.4; SL.1.1, SL.1.2; L.1.1, L.1.2, L.1.6

TODAY BEGINS THE THIRD BEND in the road of this unit. Always, the first session in a new bend, like the first session in a new unit, will be an especially invitational one. You are welcoming children into the new work and helping them feel at home.

For this next bend, you'll convey to children that writers the world over look to the work of other authors as a source of insight and instruction. Just as aspiring ballplayers study the moves of pro ball players, your children will study the moves authors make. You'll introduce this concept by returning to the story you shared at the start of the unit, *Night of the Veggie Monster*, or another mentor text you have chosen for your students. Whereas earlier, you and the children read and admired the story, emulating its Small Moments structure, now the class will return to it, intent on learning specific craft moves from George and, after this session, on transferring those moves to their own writing. If you engage children in a mentor text study, children will see a surprising number of admirable features—and learn the value of looking closely.

In today's session, you will get started. You will coach students to find and think about (and even begin to emulate) special features in a mentor text. Of course, it is not necessarily the case that just because George McClements's story benefits from ellipses, the stories written by all the writers in your class will also benefit from that particular punctuation. Brace yourself, because you're apt to find that today leads to a proliferation of ellipses. You'll be right to question whether that craft move actually improves every child's story (it won't), but the important thing is for you to keep your eye on the real goal. The goal is not that writers add ellipses or exact action words or any other specific craft move to their writing. The real goal is that writers see the books they read as sources for lessons in the craft of writing well, that they notice not only what authors say, but also how they write, and say, "I could try that in my writing, too!" You will be inviting children to tap into a never-ending resource—books.

Studying a Story to Learn Ways the Author Makes It Special

CONNECTION

Talk about people emulating a famous athlete to rally children to understand the value of studying and emulating professionals.

"Have any of you ever watched a pro soccer player and seen him or her do something special, and thought, 'I'm going to try to do that?'" Hands shot up. The soccer fans in the class were with me. "When you study what a great athlete does and then try that same thing yourself, you are doing what writers do all the time."

❖ **Name the teaching point.**

"Writers read books written by other authors and say, 'Oh my goodness! He just did something special in his book that I want to try in my *own* writing!' And then they try it."

TEACHING

Demonstrate studying a mentor author, naming specific moves he made that make his Small Moment story so special, and then emulating those moves.

"We are also going to do that today—study a writer and try out a way he writes.

"Do you remember long ago at the very start of this unit when you first heard me read aloud the Small Moment story we now know so well, *Night of the Veggie Monster*? How many of you thought, 'I wonder if I can write Small Moment stories like that?'

"Well, give yourselves a big pat on the back, stand up, and take a bow, because yes, indeed, you have written Small Moment stories like that one!" As children took their bows, I applauded their hard work. "Bravo! We've already started doing this work of looking at books to help us write like great authors. But here's the thing: there's so much more we can learn.

"Since we already know a lot from this one book, we're going to have to really study it closely like we have been studying our rock collection to learn even more. Today's minilesson, then, isn't going to be the same as most days. Most days,

◆ COACHING

This session focuses on one of the most natural ways writers have for improving their craft. They study the texts they love. It is no exaggeration to say that writers have always learned from great authors they admire. Whether they are writing The Color Purple *or* Harold's Purple Crayon, *every author writes with her heroes in mind. Models of excellence are powerful. How many tiny athletes have charged across their living room with a ball after watching their team score a winning touchdown on TV, thinking to themselves, "I can be just like that"? So while your young writers are probably not yet ready to pen a bestseller, it is important, even essential, that they believe they can.*

Today you will help children through studying a mentor text carefully, noticing the craft moves the author makes. In the next few days, you'll help children focus more fully on trying those same moves in their own writing—though they may end up diving in and trying out some craft moves today too!

I teach you something about good writing, and then we all try it out on the carpet, and then you try it in your writing at some point when it makes sense to do so. But *today* George McClements is going to be our teacher." I held up the enlarged version of the text. "Today we are going to learn from George together.

"Writers, today we are *all* (me included) going to try to answer the question, 'What does George McClements do to make *Night of The Veggie Monster* so special?' And then tomorrow and in future writing times we'll be able to try it in our own writing. This is something writers do all the time—study texts closely to learn from the ways other writers have written and eventually try what they've learned in their own writing!

"As I read, watch how I notice what, exactly, George has done that makes this one small moment—this ordinary every-day moment—so special!"

> *It all starts when I'm forced to eat . . .*

As I read, I pretended to reluctantly touch a pea and then made a face, modeling for kids how to put themselves into the moment as a reader. Switching out of the acting role, I said, "Writers, I'm noticing something."

> *It all starts when I'm forced to eat . . .*

I let my voice trail off before exclaiming,

> *PEAS!*
>
> *With just the slightest touch . . .*

Again, I let my voice trail off.

> *It begins.*

"Wow. See how George changed how we read this and got us excited by putting in those three dots? George *could* have just written, 'It all starts when I'm forced to eat *peas*!'" I said in a rush. "And 'With just the slightest touch it begins.'" Again, I said this in a rush. "But *instead*, he wrote those dots (writers call them *ellipses*) to tell us to wait a few seconds before reading on. It's like George is signaling to his reader, 'Listen up! Here comes an important part!' and that gets us excited to find out what's next.

"Let's start a chart and list this as the first special craft move authors do that we can do too."

Learning Craft Moves from a Mentor Author

What did George McClements do?	Why did he do this?
Wrote ELLIPSES in the middle of the sentence	To build excitement

"Let's keep reading."

"Oh, here's something else George did. He wrote the *exact* actions the little boy took with his body: the little boy's toes *twist* and *curl up* in his shoes. He *squirms* in his seat. He starts to *transform*." I emphasized the action words *twist, curl, squirm,* and *transform,* twisting my feet and squirming in my seat, and making a monster face and hands. "What great words to describe exactly what is going on for that little boy! George could have written, 'My body doesn't like it when I eat the pea,' but that wouldn't have had the same effect. All those exact actions George wrote really pull me into the story and help make a movie in my mind. Let's add that to our chart."

What did George McClements do?	Why did he do this?
Wrote ELLIPSES in the middle of the sentence	To build excitement
Wrote EXACT ACTIONS that people do	To make a movie in the reader's mind

Debrief. Name what you have demonstrated in a way that is transferable to other texts and other days.

"Writers, see how I read *Night of the Veggie Monster* just now, really studying it closely, like we do our rock collection? And how I asked myself, 'What are the special things the author, George McClements, did that I could try too?'"

ACTIVE ENGAGEMENT

Ask children to follow along as you read aloud the story from beginning to end. Give them sticky notes to put on the parts of the text where they notice the mentor author doing something special.

"Writers, it's your turn now. I'm giving each of you some sticky notes and copies of this story. I'm going to read it aloud from beginning to end one more time, and as I do, really study it with your eyes and your ears. *Look* and *listen* for the special things you notice George has done. When you notice something special, put a sticky note on that part."

Read aloud the whole story, emphasizing the bold and all-caps words, the ellipses, and the actions.

"Turn and show your partner the parts you stickered just now. Talk about why those parts felt special to you and try your best to name what George did. I'm going to eavesdrop as you talk, to see if I can help."

As partners talked, I listened in, coaching into their conversations as needed.

Share what children notice, rephrasing as needed to explain the craft moves.

"Writers, listen to the things *you* noticed that George did in this part to make the story special. Amanda and Sarah noticed that George wrote really big words. Look. Here and here." I pointed to *PEAS* and *GULP*. "Yes, George played around a little by making those big, and he also wrote them in all capital letters. And Maxwell and Brendan noticed that

Your student may notice something else you could share. Or, you can let them know children in another class noticed these moves.

some words are really dark." I pointed to some of the words in bold. "Let's call them 'pop-out' words because they look almost like they pop out of the page.

"Great observing, writers! George *did* write with lots of capital, dark (bold) words. I wonder why he wrote those pop-out words. Turn and talk to your partner again about why you think he did that.

"Give me a thumbs up if you have ideas."

"He wrote them so we would read them strong!" Maxwell exclaimed.

"We do read these words extra strong, don't we? And look, he used those in the first part of his story, too." I pointed to the opening lines of the story.

"I bet all of you could try that out in your own writing. I'll add 'words that pop out' to our chart, and I will write that he did that so we know to read those words strong and with excitement."

Learning Craft Moves from a Mentor Author

What did George McClements do?	Why did he do this?
Wrote ELLIPSES in the middle of a sentence	To build up excitement
Wrote EXACT ACTIONS that people do	To make a movie in the reader's mind
Wrote some words that POP OUT	To tell the reader to read with a strong voice

Debrief, reminding writers to transfer what they have learned to their own writing.

"So, writers, here is the important thing. We can study texts we love to learn new ways to write! Our favorite writers can be our favorite writing teachers! We just need to read and reread their writing, asking ourselves, 'What made this part of the writing so special?' and 'What has this writer done that I could try?'"

LINK

Set writers up to find even more craft moves from the mentor text—or another favorite story—that they could try in their own writing.

"Today, and every day, you can look to your favorite books for special things to try in your own writing. Also, like writers always do, you can invent your own way of making your writing special! I'm passing out booklets. Take a minute and plan what you will work on today. You might be starting a new story or continuing with one you've been working on. You might also want to study a mentor text today, finding more special craft moves that you want to try out in your own writing. You have lots of choices for writing time today. I can't wait to see what craft moves you find or try out in your writing!"

120

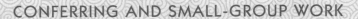

Helping Writers Use Audience and Purpose to Decide Which Craft Moves to Emulate

YOUR MESSAGE TODAY IS NOT THAT IT IS IMPORTANT to include big, bold words and ellipses, but instead, that it is important to study mentor texts. So you'll want to continue this theme by using your conferences and small-group work for children to do their own observing and their own naming of what works in this text or other mentor texts, and to think about how—and for what purpose—they might try out these techniques in their own writing.

At this point in the year, it is a great time to help writers begin to give more thought to their audience and purpose for writing, connecting the strategies they are trying out in their writing with *who* they are writing for. When they have an audience in mind and know what it is they want those readers to know (even if it is something as simple as "I want them to know it was so much fun" or "It was so scary"), then they write with greater intention, beginning to understand the effect the details they are including and techniques they are trying have on their reader.

As you pull up next to a writer and notice him trying out a strategy, you'll want to spend the first part of the conference discovering what the child is working on. "What are you working on as a writer?" you'll ask. We ask this often, and with young children we often get a response that describes the content of a story, rather than the writer's process. You can use this opportunity to nudge him toward naming what he is doing. You might begin by having him name an audience. Is he writing this for a friend? His writing partner? His mom? His cousin? Once the audience is established, you can then elicit the writer's purpose by asking, "What do you want the reader to know, think, or feel?" When the writer responds, "I want him to know it was so, so fun to go on the ride," you can help him see what he has already done to convey this to the reader. "I can see you are the kind of writer who really shows how you were feeling. Here you wrote, 'This is fun!' What else might you try out in your writing to show your reader that the ride was fun? Is there anything one of our mentor authors did that you could try?" You may need to nudge the writer to look at the "Learning Craft Moves from a Mentor Author" chart or at his copy of the mentor text for ideas. The child might say,

MID-WORKSHOP TEACHING
Finding Another Writing Move to Emulate

"Writers, I love how you just dove right in to find things this writer did that you could try in your own writing. John found something very important about George McClements that we didn't talk about yet. Let's count the number of lines George wrote on this page when the boy turns into the veggie monster." We counted together. "He wrote four lines on one page! He is the kind of writer who pushes himself to write as much as he can, building up his writing muscles. The key is that he didn't just write more and fill it with any silly words. He wrote four lines staying in the small moment about the boy eating the pea. John found that in George McClements's work and he is going to try that too."

"I could add the actions I did. I put my hands in the air. And I screamed." To which you could reply, "Write that down. And remember, anytime you want to show your reader how you are feeling, you can add actions to your story. This is a technique that many authors use in their writing."

Expect that it will be a challenge for many children to transfer the craft moves they notice in a published text to their own writing. Some children may recall a move and replicate it but fail to understand its purpose. For example, a child may add ellipses that do not build excitement or tension. Don't worry too much at this stage if children misuse a strategy. All of us do this when we are learning something new and we will focus on transference in the next few sessions. However, *do* keep asking your writers to think about *why* they chose to use a particular strategy and what effect it might have on their reader. In time, they will begin to use craft moves purposefully, in ways that improve their writing.

Noticing Craft Moves in Our Writing

Ask the class to function as a student's partner. Ask students to listen and look at the piece, raising a finger each time they notice a craft move they could try too.

"Class, as I was conferring, I saw so many of you writing those special things in your stories that we noticed in *Night of the Veggie Monster*. Eliza doesn't have a partner today, so let's all pretend that we are her partner. The first time she reads it, let's all listen to her story. Then, the second time she reads it, put a finger up each time you hear or see something she did that made her writing special that you could try." I signaled to the craft chart we had just created in the minilesson. Eliza read her story aloud, holding her booklet outward, so the class could follow along. (See Figure 14–1.)

After Eliza read her story, I said "I see so many fingers raised. What is one special thing Eliza did in her writing like George?"

Shariff said, "She made bold words and they are big! She said those with a *loud* voice."

"Great noticing! Did anyone notice another craft move you could try?" I turned back to the first page.

"She used those three dots," Cooper announced.

"Yes," I said, "she used an ellipsis to make us wonder what was going to happen on the airplane!"

End by asking the children to turn and talk, doing this work now independently.

"Wow—you noticed what Eliza did that you could try! Now read your partner's story. The second time you hear it, raise a finger each time you hear or see a craft move in your partner's story that you could try."

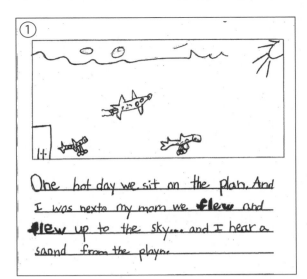

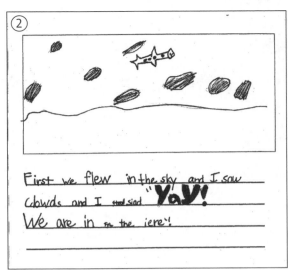

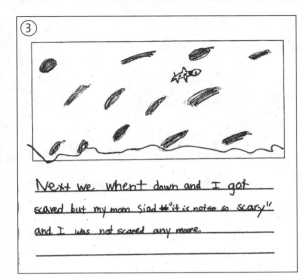

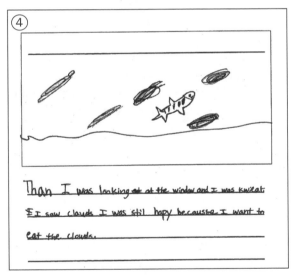

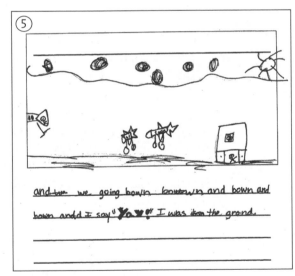

Page 1: One hot day we sat on the plane. And I was next to my mom. We flew and flew up to the sky. . . . and I hear a sound from the plane.

Page 2: First we flew in the sky and I saw clouds and I said "Yay!" We are in the air!

Page 3: Next we went down and I got scared but my mom said, "It is not so scary," and I was not scared anymore.

Page 4: Then I was looking out the window and I was quiet. I saw clouds. I was still happy because I want to eat the clouds.

Page 5: And we were going down down and down and down and I say "Yay!" I was on the the ground.

FIG. 14–1 Eliza's story about flying in an airplane with craft moves similar to those found in the class mentor text

Trying Out a Craft Move
from a Mentor Text

Writing with Exact Actions

IN THIS SESSION, you'll teach children that once writers have discovered a craft move to emulate, they try it out in their own writing. In this case, they could try out helping their readers make a movie in their mind, drawing them into the story by including the exact actions of their characters.

GETTING READY

✔ The mentor text, *Night of the Veggie Monster* (or whatever text you've selected), enlarged or displayed, to study as a class

✔ "Learning Craft Moves from a Mentor Author" chart (see Teaching)

✔ A 3-page booklet with sketches of a shared class experience and a rather flat first sentence that you'll use to demonstrate today's instruction (see Teaching and Active Engagement)

✔ Writing partners should sit next to each other for writing time

TODAY YOU'LL TEACH CHILDREN that close study of a text pays off; the craft moves they discover in the texts they read become strategies to try in their own writing. The teaching in this session and the next—and indeed any sessions involving children learning from mentor texts—is double-layered. For one, you are teaching children the process of learning about writing from a mentor text, and for another, you are teaching children about the particular craft move they've chosen.

In the previous session, you helped students notice what stood out to them in George McClements's story, and also helped them see why these particular craft moves were used. That is, you coached them through the process of studying a mentor text. Today, you'll help children learn to take the results of that close study to their own writing.

In this session, you will use the example of one craft move, writing with exact actions, and you will give your writers more practice transferring this skill to their own writing. Specifically, you will suggest that exact action words have the power to bring readers into the story, to envision the scene and experience it firsthand. The goal is for children to learn to take what they have learned in a mentor text and to use it in their own work, in this case, learning to write using more precise action words, knowing that doing so will give their reader a mental picture of the action.

COMMON CORE STATE STANDARDS: W.1.3, W.1.5; RL.1.1, RL.1.4; SL.1.1, ; L.1.1, L.1.2, L.1.5.d

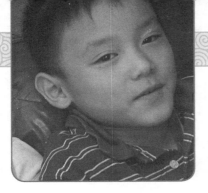

Trying Out a Craft Move from a Mentor Text
Writing with Exact Actions

CONNECTION

Help children remember all they've learned in the unit that can help them bring their stories to life.

"Do you know the story *Frankenstein*? It is a *very* famous story written by a woman named Mary Shelley. In this book, a scientist built a person from spare parts and, of course, the person he built had no life in him at all. There was nothing special about the creature. He was just lying there, lifeless. The scientist wanted to give the creature life, so he had to think and think and think. Finally he came up with a strategy, and this was it: electricity. He decided to use electricity to give his creature life. And it happened. He got electricity to bring this being alive. You'll have to read it yourself to find out what happens, but here's what I am going to ask you: what strategies are you using to bring *your* work to life? What are you going to use as electricity for your writing? Turn and tell your partner." As children talked, I pointed soundlessly at the chart of ways to bring your writing to life, to help those who were at a loss and needed some reminders.

Students found this craft move last session, now you can show them why they looked for it in the first place: to help their writing come alive!

"I heard some of you naming some of the items on our chart and some of you talking about new ways you've thought of. I also heard some of you naming some ways we saw in George's writing from last workshop. Today I want to work with you more on one of those strategies we found from studying our mentor text: describing exact actions."

Name the teaching point.

"Today I want to teach you that when writers want to make their stories really special they can turn to craft moves they've learned from studying mentor authors. Once they've found a move that fits their purpose, they can try it in their own writing. One craft move writers use is telling the exact actions people do."

TEACHING

Highlight the craft move you want children to notice in the mentor text, emphasizing the purpose for this technique. In this case, point out that exact action words help readers envision the story.

"Let's reread part of *Night of the Veggie Monster* again and listen for the descriptions of exact actions that George uses. When you hear the book describing the small, exact actions that a person does, the craft move we found last time, give me a thumbs up." I began to read.

> *My fingers become all wiggly.*
>
> *As the pea rests in my mouth, my eyes begin to water.*
>
> *My toes twist and curl up in my shoes.*

A handful of kids put their thumbs up. "You are right. George didn't just say, 'I moved around in my chair.' Instead, he described the exact actions. His toes twist and curl up in his shoes.

"And here is the important thing. Those actions show us something about exactly how the boy moved, don't they? I feel like when I copy what those exact moves were—for real or in my imagination—I am disgusted with something just like he is! I twist and curl my toes in my own shoes, and it almost makes me make a disgusted face, because the two go together so much—that exact action and the disgust he's feeling! It's really true that the exact actions make the story come alive, because those exact actions bring other feelings or actions into my mind that aren't even there. They make the story do things to me!" I acted out the scene, carefully, and let the disgust show on my face.

Demonstrate using small, exact action words in a shared class story.

"This craft move we found is so powerful, we've got to try it ourselves! Let me try it on the story I'm planning to write about last week's party. Here's what I have so far." I showed the children a three-page booklet with sketches of the dance party and these words.

> One afternoon I told the class, "I have a surprise for you. Let's meet on the rug." I went to the rug and waited for the kids to come and sit.

"I could keep that, but I want to make this story come alive—give it some electricity by using exact actions. What exactly happened? Let me try to remember. I was sitting there like this." I demonstrated remembering back to the moment, and as I reenacted it I rubbed my hands together in remembered excitement. As I did so, I suddenly stopped rubbing my hands together and held them up in the air and exclaimed, "That is an exact action I did! Now I remember! How about this?

> I told the class, "I have a surprise for you. Let's meet on the rug." I WENT over to the rug and sat in my chair, rubbing my hands together as I waited for the kids to come and sit.

I wrote it quickly. "Now, before I move to the next part, let me think about exactly what I did next. I was so excited, my body was definitely not still. Hmm." I closed my eyes, pictured it in my mind, and then started to move my body as I had done that day. "Oh, that's right, I was smiling really big and I put my hand over my mouth so I wouldn't say the surprise too soon. I could write":

> I SMILED as the kids sat down on the rug. I COVERED my mouth with my hand so that I would
> not tell the surprise too soon.

"Yes, that's it! Now I've written the exact actions—exactly how I moved, so anyone who reads it will see the movie in their mind, almost feeling like they were right there with us when I was about to reveal the surprise!" I wrote the sentences quickly and then turned to the next page.

Debrief, reminding writers of the purpose of the day's teaching point.

"Wow! Did you notice how I asked myself, 'What exactly did I do?' and I came up with some changes?" Those action words bring life and electricity to the story. Writers use exact actions to bring their stories to life, pulling readers in by giving them movies in their minds." I pointed to the "Learning Craft Moves from a Mentor Author" chart where this had been recorded the previous day.

ACTIVE ENGAGEMENT

Have the children turn and talk to help you continue to write the shared class story, using small, exact action words.

"Writers, I need your help to write the next page of the story. Here is the sketch I made of when I showed you the bubble wrap. Picture *exactly* what happened next. What exactly did I do? What did you do? Put one finger up for each action you remember." I waited as the children recounted the story in their minds. Some children closed their eyes. Others whispered as they touched their fingers. "Okay, turn and tell your partner what we should write next." The children turned to their partners and rattled off the rest of the event.

"Put a thumb on your knee if you want to tell me what happened next." I called on a kid.

"You told us we were going to have a dance party on the roll of bubble wrap," Emily said.

"Yes, Emily, I did tell you that," I said. "Now think of an action word that describes *exactly* how I told you. Turn and talk again. Tell your partner how you would describe that exact action." After a few seconds, I reconvened the class. "Who has an exact action word to describe how I told you about the dance party?"

Rachel chimed in, "You leaned over and *whispered* to us."

Notice how I slow the process down, showing each step I take to come up with the words I use. You will want to do the same in your demonstrations. Remember your writers need to learn not only what the strategy is and why it is important but also exactly how to use it.

"Great! I am going to write that."

I leaned over and whispered to the class, "We're going to have a dance party."

"Writers, do you see how the small action," I leaned over and whispered as I said this, "makes a reader feel almost as if she's in on our bubble party herself! Like she's right there with all of us, about to join in the fun! It makes a movie in the reader's mind—and gets the reader excited!"

LINK

Suggest that children try out this craft move today in their own writing, and tell them that they can always use it when they want to help readers envision their stories.

"Writers, today and every day, I hope you'll remember that when you discover a craft move, when you discover a way a writer made his or her work special, you can try it yourself! And also, I hope you'll remember this special craft move we learned from George: Writers write exact action words to draw their readers into the story. I bet lots of you are going to want to try a craft move you've found or even this exact craft move in your writing today! Great! Off you go!"

Coaching Small Groups in Using Exact Action Words

YOU MAY FIND THAT MANY OF YOUR CHILDREN enthusiastically tackle this craft move, revising their stories to add small actions to help readers create a movie in their minds. Other children may reread their stories and feel unsure of where they could try out this craft move. Some may have a difficult time generating precise small actions to use in their stories. Others may try out other craft moves or take on different writing work altogether.

As always, the most important teaching of the day may not be related to the minilesson, but if children are trying to include small actions to draw readers into their stories, you can help. Call together a small group of children who need support:

"Writers, I brought you together today because I noticed that you have all written stories with lots of action. Cooper wrote about building a blanket fort, and Sarah wrote about making cupcakes, for example. Because your stories are so full of big actions, I think you're ready to try out using exact words to also show small actions that draw readers in. I'll show you what I mean with my story."

> One day I was at the beach with my grandpa. I was excited to swim. I went into the water.

"Now I'll rewind that memory to remember exactly what actions I did. Close your eyes and try to make a movie in your mind with me. So I didn't just go to the water. Playing it in slow motion in my mind, 'I kicked off my flip flops. I threw my hat on the sand and dashed to the water.' Do you see that movie in your mind?" The kids nodded. "Open your eyes, see how I didn't just say 'I went in the water'? I remembered the small, *exact* actions I did to show how I went in."

> One day I was at the beach with my grandpa. I kicked off my flip flops and threw my hat on the sand. I dashed to the water.

"Do you see how I pictured the exact small actions I did and added those to my writing, so the reader can picture them too? Now, try it in your stories, right here!"

I prompted students as I moved around the semicircle. Sarah was thinking about her action, "I ate the cupcake." "Act that out in your mind. How did it go as you were eating it?"

After a moment, Sarah said, "I licked the frosting off the top, first. I'll put that!"

After a few minutes, I brought the group's attention back to me. "What acting! Listen to how Sarah used an exact action word today. First she wrote, 'I ate the cupcake.' Then, she changed it to, 'I *licked* the frosting off the top, first.' Doesn't that help you picture it? So, writers, remember that you can add more small actions to your stories by acting out what happened in your mind and then writing down what you see, using the exact words to describe the action. Off you go to continue writing!"

MID-WORKSHOP TEACHING Partners Story-Tell Twice, the Second Time for More Precise, Exact Action Words

"Writers, it is challenging and fun work to write not just what you did, but the *exact* actions you did. Partners are the best tool for doing this well, and that is why you are sitting next to each other as you write. Partner 1, first tell your partner your story across your fingers. Partner 2, see if you can picture your partner's story in your mind. If there is action that you can't quite picture, tell your partner where adding exact action words might help.

"Now, tell your story *a second time* but this time use more exact action words in the places your partner suggested. Change some of your action words so that you tell your partner exactly what you did."

Trying Out Another Found Craft Move

Remind students that they can read a mentor text and think, "I could try that in my writing." Offer up an example of a student who has done that.

"You guys have learned so much from George. *Night of the Veggie Monster* has become another writing teacher for you! A few days ago when we all reread the text together, many of you noticed the three dots together, the ellipses. Remember?"

> *I* **squirm** *in my seat. I try to keep control but the* **pea** *is too strong. I start to transform into . . .*

As I read this I paused and let the dramatic excitement and suspense build.

> *a VEGGIE MONSTER!*

"And, since we talked about it yesterday, you all know that when you notice something an author does you can try it in your own writing. So, guess what? Since we noticed the ellipses, Ariel tried them! Isn't that a great idea she had? She put some ellipses in her own story for the same reason George did—to build excitement. Here is what she had first written." I had this written on chart paper already and now revealed it to them.

> My friend was coming to visit from far away. I went to the airport to pick her up. I waited and waited and waited. Finally, she came off the plane and I ran to give her a hug.

"Then she thought, 'I want to build excitement. I was so excited! Where can I use the ellipses?' Turn and tell your partner where you think she put them."

Turning to her partner, Emma said, "After 'my friend.'"

"No," Maxwell said. "Then it'd go, 'My friend . . . was coming. . . .' I think it should be after the word *waited*."

Share one partnership's thinking with the class.

"I just heard Liam suggest that the piece could go, 'I waited . . . and waited . . . and waited. . . .' Does that sound like a good place to add ellipses and build suspense?"

The children chorused, "Yeees."

"Well, it certainly helps us feel Ariel's building excitement while she waits! I can tell she's excited to find out what will happen when her friend gets there, and I get the feeling she thinks her friend is never going to come! Doesn't it always feel like that when something you really want to happen is about to happen but it feels like it is taking forever? Like it takes forever to get to your birthday?"

Ask children to experiment with ellipses quickly, there on the rug. Suggest that others may try other strategies and techniques that interest them.

"Just for a second, now, look over the writing you did today and see if there is a spot where George can teach you something. Is there a place where you want to build excitement and you could add ellipses? Is there a place where you want the reader to really envision what you are writing about, so you could insert a small action? Is there something else that George (or another writer) has done that you could use to help your own writing? Talk with your partner about this for a moment before we end writing workshop for today. If you figure something out, mark the spot on your page so you can remember to do it next workshop!"

Trying Out a Craft Move from a Mentor Text
Writing with Pop-Out Words

IN THIS SESSION, you'll teach children that once writers have discovered a craft move to emulate, they try it out in their own writing. In this case, they could try out giving their readers clues about how to read their story, including writing words bigger and bolder for emphasis.

GETTING READY

✔ A copy of the mentor text, *Night of the Veggie Monster*, or whatever text you've selected

✔ "Learning Craft Moves from a Mentor Author" chart

✔ Copy of the mentor text for each child to sit on until you read it aloud (see Teaching)

✔ Students' writing folders and pencils for the minilesson (see Active Engagement)

✔ A student's piece with pop-out words to demonstrate reading with expression (see Share)

T HE LAST TWO SESSIONS have focused on closely studying a mentor text and looking for craft moves to emulate. As your children have been learning from other authors, they are getting used to the idea of borrowing great ideas from the books and authors they love, using these craft moves to enhance their writing. It is valuable to continue this study today, giving students yet more opportunities to learn from their favorite authors and to bravely experiment in their own writing with what they have found, including using ellipses, bolds, capitals, and action words.

In this session, you'll help children try out yet another craft move they've likely discovered: writers choose words they want to emphasize and highlight by writing them big and bold. The words can be so obvious to the reader, they almost pop out of the page; hence, "pop-out words." Writers can decide the size, shape, boldness, and spacing between these words to convey certain reading voices and emotions. These words help the reader read in a "storytelling voice."

In this session, your children will investigate why George McClements chose to write certain words big and bold, giving them more opportunities to hone their skill of naming why an author might use a particular craft move in his or her text. Then you will demonstrate how to use this craft move with the shared class story. Children will then have the chance to practice using this craft move in their own writing by going back and adding pop-out words to a piece they have already written. Students should leave today confident that they can emulate any craft move they find in their favorite authors' texts, learning along the way how to string words across the page to engage the reader's best storytelling voice.

COMMON CORE STATE STANDARDS: W.1.3, W.1.5; RL.1.1, RL.1.4, RFS.1.4.b; SL.1.1, SL.1.6; L.1.1, L.1.2

Trying Out a Craft Move from a Mentor Text
Writing with Pop-Out Words

CONNECTION

Remind children of the ways the mentor author brings his text to life.

"Writers, you have been learning so many craft moves from studying mentor texts like *Night of the Veggie* Monster. And, you've been trying them out in your own writing, too! Right now, will you turn to your partner and name some of the craft moves you've discovered and some you've tried?" I gave them a moment and gestured to our charts for any students who seemed stumped.

It's important that children have this chance to recall the craft moves they've learned in this bend so that they're able to transfer these moves to their own writing.

❖ **Name the teaching point.**

"Today I am going to remind you that writers don't just *notice* craft moves other writers use, they *try* them! For example, we found that writers make some words big, bold, and different shapes to show that these words are important to the story and should be read in a strong voice. Since we noticed that, let's try that in our own writing."

TEACHING

Research the mentor text, discussing the reason why the author would use this craft move.

"Every one of you has a copy of *Night of the Veggie Monster* under your legs now. I want you to listen and follow along as I reread the book again. Notice how the big, bold words, the pop-out words, help me read the story." I read a section of the story, emphasizing the bold words with a strong, dramatic voice.

Channel children to summarize their observations.

"Talk to someone next to you about how big, bold words help us understand and read the story." The room erupted in chatter.

"I hear many of you saying that the author is telling me to use a strong voice—not a scream, but a strong voice—by writing pop-out words. I also heard you

Learning Craft Moves from a Mentor Author

What did George McClements do?	Why did he do this?
Wrote ELLIPSES in the middle of a sentence	To build up excitement
Wrote EXACT ACTIONS that people do	To make a movie in the reader's mind.
Wrote some words that POP OUT	To tell the reader to read with a strong voice

say that the author uses pop-out words to show the reader that these words are important to the story. He wants us to hear the feelings in his words!"

Reread your shared class story, demonstrating how to revise for big and bold words.

"I am going to reread my story about our class dance party, and I am going to look for places where I could make some words pop out. So as I read, I have to think: which words are really important in my story? Which words should the reader say in a strong voice?" Pointing under each word in my booklet for the children to follow, I read my story aloud in a steady, monotone voice.

> One afternoon I told the class, "I have a surprise for you. Let's meet on the rug." I went over to
> the rug and sat in my chair, rubbing my hands together as I waited for the kids to come and sit.
> They all sped over as fast as they could. I smiled as the kids sat down on the rug. I covered my
> mouth with my hand so that I would not tell the surprise too soon.
> I unraveled a giant piece of bubble wrap on the rug. I leaned over and whispered to the class,
> "We're going to have a dance party."
> Pop, Pop, Pop! We all jumped and danced around on the bubbles.

I thought aloud, "Hmm, let's see. Well, the word *surprise* is really important to what happened in my story. I want them to know how excited I felt, so I am going to go over the word *surprise* with my pencil a few times to make it big and bold. I think *giant* is another important word. I am going to go back and make that word big and bold. I also noticed George wrote the word *slightest* with big spaces between the letters to really streeetch out that word. Well, I want to try to change the spaces of my letters with the word *sped*. I want the reader to read that fast so instead of putting big spaces between the letters in that word, I am going to write those letters extra, extra close. That will tell my reader to read it super fast.

"Let's listen to how different our story sounds now." We reread the story together, using dramatic voices to emphasize the big, bold words.

> One afternoon I told the class, "I have a **SURPRISE** for you. Let's meet on the rug." I went over
> to the rug and sat in my chair, rubbing my hands together as I waited for the kids to come and
> sit.
> They all **SPED** over as fast as they could. I smiled as the kids sat down on the rug. I covered my
> mouth with my hand so that I would not tell the surprise too soon.
> I unraveled a **GIANT** piece of bubble wrap on the rug. I leaned over and whispered to the class,
> "We're going to have a dance party."
> Pop, Pop, Pop! We all jumped and danced around on the bubbles.

When we demonstrate asking ourselves questions when applying a strategy, we give students a tool they can use when writing independently. We hope that these questions are ones they internalize through our modeling and coaching.

Debrief, reminding writers to look for important words in their stories that they want readers to read in a strong voice.

"Writers, did you see how I reread my story and then asked myself, 'What words are really important in my story? What words do I want the reader to read in a strong voice?' When I found those words, I revised by writing them big and bold so that they pop out."

ACTIVE ENGAGEMENT

Ask children to take a finished piece from their folders, reread it, and then revise it with pop-out words.

"Writers, open your folder and take out a story from the finished side of your folder. Reread your story and think, 'What words are really important? What words do I want my reader to read in a strong voice?' Make those special words big and bold by writing over them a few times with a pencil so that they pop out of your story."

LINK

Remind children that they can use the craft moves they've discovered, including using big and bold words, in their writing when they write and also when they revise. Then send them off to write.

"Writers, today and every day, you can use the craft moves you discover! For example, you can write pop-out words in your stories. Pop-out words make it easier to understand important ideas and feelings. You can also use pop-out words when you revise a story, rewriting the words, changing their size, and changing the spaces between the letters.

"Take a minute now to think, writers. Are you continuing a piece from yesterday or starting a new piece? Will you try a craft move? Give me a thumbs up when you have your plan.

"Let's get started," I said, as the last thumb popped up.

It is important that children know that all the craft and elaboration strategies we teach them can be used as they write new pieces or when they revise or even when they are planning. In a minilesson, we often demonstrate the use of the strategy (or strategies) in one stage of the process, and we want to make sure writers know other times they can also do that work.

Supporting Writers Using Craft Moves through the Writing Process

T HOUGH OF COURSE CHILDREN ARE FREE TO DO THE WRITING WORK they need to do and to try any craft move at all, they will be very eager to add pop-out words. As you know, during read-alouds, they love to join in and read the big, bold words with a strong voice. Since this is the third session supporting the use of craft moves learned from mentor authors, it is important that writers are able to use this newfound craft while continuing to move through the writing process. Your goal is to ensure that students understand that they can incorporate these moves into planning, drafting, revising, and even editing.

You may want to work with children who need support rehearsing their stories. Some may still need support in telling a cohesive and sequential story, while others are ready to incorporate craft moves such as adding dialogue, feelings, and exact actions into their story from the beginning of the process—during the storytelling. You can sit with them and coach them as they touch and tell their stories across pages or across their fingers.

Children who are either overusing or not using craft moves they've discovered will benefit from support with moving from sketching to writing words, thinking carefully about where to include these moves before writing. Imagine, for example, a child who is writing every word big and bold. Have the writer tell you how that page will go. When you notice his voice get louder and excited, you can stop him and point out just that word. "Did you hear how you said *balloon* with such a strong, excited voice when you were telling it to me? That would be a great word to make pop out so that the reader would know to read it just like that."

While you hope that children reread their writing to make sure it makes sense before putting it in the finished side of the folder, you will inevitably find writers who need support monitoring for sense *as* they write. This becomes especially important as their stories become more detailed. Some kids may lose the meaning of the story as they try out all of these new craft moves. Possibly in a small-group lesson, teach such children that writers only try craft moves that make sense for a particular story. You can model

---

MID-WORKSHOP TEACHING
Writers Draw Their Letters to Show Us What Words Mean

"Writers, may I stop you? Ian noticed the coolest thing that I have to share with you! Ian had his copy of *Night of the Veggie Monsters* next to him as he reread his story so that he could take new ideas from it. Guess what he found? George writes some important pop-out words by writing them big and bold, *but* he also draws some of his letters so that the words *look* like what they mean."

I held up the book, pointing out several examples. "Let's look. He writes 'My toes **TWIST** and **CURL UP**.'

"*Up* curls up in text. Then here he writes 'I **SQUIRM** in my seat.' The letters seem to wiggle. And in another example here, he says, 'Ready to tip.' The letters lean forward, as if tipping.

"Do you see, writers, how George has drawn the letters in his action words so that they act out what the word means? For *up*, the letters go up. For *tip*, the letters look like they are tipping. For *squirm*, the letters seem to wiggle on the page like worms. What a clever trick! Writers, you can do this in your stories, too. As you write, you can draw your words in different ways to make moving words look like they really move! This is another way you can help readers read your story, just like a professional writer. Keep going."

---

cramming all of the craft moves the class has studied into every line of your story. Then point out that instead of bringing your story to life, all that cramming caused your story to be disconnected. Model rereading to make sure your writing makes sense, and then take out certain parts.

Reading Aloud to Revise

Tell children that writers act like readers, using their voice to show how the words are written and to show feelings.

After calling writers back to the meeting area, asking them to sit with their partners, I said, "Writers, we have learned that when we read, we change our voices for different parts of the story. For example, when we see quotation marks, we change our voices to sound like the person talking. When we see ellipses, we pause. We read pop-out words in a loud, excited way. Not a scream," I modeled that in an exaggerated way, "but a strong voice." I modeled that too.

Read aloud a student's piece to demonstrate reading with expression.

(See Figure 16–1 on the next page.)

"Writers, did you hear how my voice changed at the really exciting part? I did that because Ronald signaled me to read with a strong voice." I turned the page around and pointed to capitalized words. "When we read it that way we can really feel the excitement Ronald felt!"

Channel children to reread their stories to their partners, practicing reading with expression.

"Now read your story to your partner, making sure you change your voice to read those big, bold words the way you meant for them to be read. As you are reading, you will probably notice something you want to change in your writing. You will probably need to change your writing to make it match how you want it to be read. Writers often do that. Try that now, with your partner!"

Children will invariably say more than they write. Partners can listen to a story and then later hear how the writer recorded the story and find a page that isn't as good as the oral version of that page. The writer and his or her partner could work together to imagine how the one page could be improved. Often revising one page leads to other revisions.

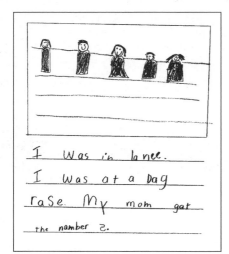

I Was in lanee.
I Was at a Dag
raSe. My mom gat
the number 5.

I was in line. I was at a dog race. My
mom got the number five.

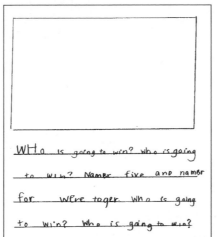

WHo is going to win? who is going
to win? Nambr five and nambr
for Were toger. Who is going
to win? Who is going to win?

Who is going to win? Who is going to
win? Number five and number four
were together. Who is going to win?
Who is going to win?

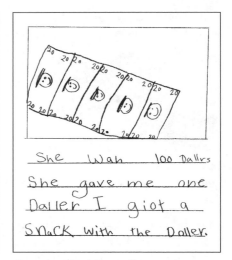

The rase startid. NumBr five Was
in the leD the rase went on for
five rasis NumBr five wan all
five rasses mY mom haD
Wan. We all shawted
YaY! We Wan!!

The race started. Number five was
in the lead. The race went on for five
races. Number five won all five races.
My mom had won. We all shouted, "Yay!
We won!"

She Wan 100 Dallrs
She gave me one
Daller I giot a
SnacK With the Daller.

She won 100 dollars. She gave me one
dollar. I got a snack with the dollar.

FIG. 16–1   Ronald's story about a dog race that highlights pop-out words

Turning to Other Mentor Texts

 Dear Teachers,

What underlies this lesson and all of the lessons in this unit is the belief that your writers have a story to tell that they can tell beautifully. The magic of children's enthusiasm should fuel this session. Scaffolding your students as they learn to question and explore new texts is not magic, however, so in this letter I offer suggestions for structuring a session to help your writers be who they want to become on the page.

Your classroom is now fully immersed in writing small moments. For the past week or so, you have taught your students to look closely at another author's writing, presumably George McClements, and you have helped them identify what George does to make his story special. You have probably been pleasantly surprised by how well the children can take an idea like "exact action words" and try to use it in their own writing. The tricky part probably has been getting them to apply new craft moves they've discovered to their work consistently and without prompting. By encouraging children to question the text you have been studying and teaching into "*Why* do you think the author does this?", you can help your writers become more independent. Once children understand the purpose of a craft move, they can say, "I want my reader to slow down and wait before reading on. Oh! I can use ellipses, like George." By expecting children to share what *they* notice about an author's writing as you introduce particular craft moves, you will set them up to question and learn from other mentor texts.

Children in this session will find their own mentor authors, study what that author has done, and try to use the craft moves they notice. This builds upon the previous sessions in the bend by recalling aspects of author study, but it stresses that *Night of the Veggie Monster* is not the key to "good" writing. Instead, children should realize that their own questions, interests, and ideas about books are powerful tools for writing well.

You might want to steer children toward books you believe will be especially helpful mentor texts. Look for texts written in such a way that children will notice and want to emulate the techniques the authors have used. You may want texts with fairly obvious

COMMON CORE STATE STANDARDS: W.1.3; RL.1.1, RL.1.4; SL.1.1; L.1.1, L.1.2

features (sound effects, print in the illustrations, a pattern to the language, and so on). Ideally, each child will identify two somewhat similar books by one author, so that she or he is engaged in an author study, not a text study. You could plan this so that pairs of children study different authors. Later you could merge these partnerships for more talk and more energy. Several authors we have found (among others) that work well are Byrd Baylor, Eric Carle, Joy Cowley, Donald Crews, Lois Ehlert, Judith Viorst, and Charlotte Zolotow.

MINILESSON

You might start by reminding the children of the craft moves they learned from George McClements. You could try to engage their interest in learning new craft moves by comparing the way different authors write to the way different people cook or skateboard or throw a baseball. In other words, everyone has a style of doing things that makes them unique. The same is true with writing. You will be encouraging your writers to find ways of using words that appeal to them. They already have favorite authors, probably, in their book bags or special corner of the classroom. You might encourage interest in particular authors by talking about your own favorites, books with accessible craft moves that you know will work well. What's important is that you get the children excited about investigating the writing of a new author the same way that they have looked at George's work.

If yesterday you taught your writers that they could show emphasis in their stories by using big bold pop-out words, today you will teach them that the ways they can enrich their own writing are as limitless as the number of books in the biggest library they can imagine. They might begin by studying authors familiar to them, bearing in mind there are always new places to look for inspiration.

You will present this focus as a clear and concise teaching point that, like others in this book, aims to instill an attitude toward writing. Try to avoid writing a teaching point that sounds like a mechanical assignment: "Today I want to teach you that you can copy things from books you like into your own writing." Commit to drafting and revising—perhaps with your colleagues—until you have worded your teaching point as a lesson the writer will always carry with her: "Today I want to teach you that writers study the books they love to find new tricks or craft moves for writing well. Writers ask, 'What does this special author do in his or her writing that I could try?'"

Then, to teach this you might want to read a book you love aloud and use Post-its to mark features of the text that stand out. You might want to think aloud each time you tag a craft move. These observations could begin with your reaction to elements of the story—"That's funny! How exciting! I wonder what will happen next?" And move through the questions you have used on your craft charts: "What is the author doing here? Why does he do this?" You could then ask partners to turn and talk about another feature they notice in the story. Students might be referred to a copy of the craft chart in your classroom for reminders about this kind of questioning. When the class regroups, your talk will circle back to the broader goal of the minilesson, that they can learn a lot about writing from the books they love.

Assuming that you have decided to pair students, you can give each partnership a different book and have students work together. Partnerships can read the stories aloud and talk about the things they like or the things that stand out to them. Children will flag text that interests them and explain what they have noticed on the Post-its. "What is the author doing here? Why?" It will be helpful to give students books they've already read so the content is familiar to them and they can spend their time examining how the author crafted the text.

Of course, when it comes to the link of your minilesson, you absolutely cannot send children off to do a set of specific actions. Mention some of the many options that are before them.

- Go back to a piece and try to use the craft moves you noticed in a new mentor text.
- Start a new piece and try to use one of the new craft moves you noticed in a new mentor text as you write.

You might send children off to work by saying, "Those of you who will be doing . . . , get started." Then, after they disperse, "Those of you who will be. . . ." You may want, as the final prompt, to say, "Those of you who are not sure what you are doing, stay here so you can help each other." This, then, collects all the lost souls and allows you to give them the support they are signaling they need.

CONFERRING AND SMALL-GROUP WORK

Your children will be at the stages of work in their new pieces that you supported in the first half of the unit, so you can scan the conferring write-ups from Sessions 5, 9, and 10 for ideas. You may want to convene all the writers who are having trouble finding a mentor text to learn from. Help them choose authors they admire and books they love by asking them to think of one book or one author from their book baggies that they have recently read. Is there a book they can't stop thinking about? An author they have read multiple books by? You might do the same to support a group of writers who need help figuring out "why the author did this in his or her writing." Help those children think about what that craft move (for example, bold words) does for that story. Does it make it more exciting? More suspenseful? What emotions do they have as readers when they see that specific craft move? If children are revising pieces by adding what they learned from their new mentor text, help them add these craft moves in places that enhance their own stories. Rather than haphazardly adding craft moves, ask writers to describe what purpose the craft move serves in their mentor author's story. Does the craft move work the same way in their story? If not, can they use it somewhere else in their story or use a different craft move? Engage students in thinking more intentionally about the moves they are trying out in their writing.

MID-WORKSHOP TEACHING

One way to set up your mid-workshop teaching is to plan on reprising an individual conference you have had for the benefit of the whole group. For example, you might praise a writer for writing with his mentor text open beside him, telling the entire class about the clever way this writer is working, encouraging them to consider this strategy.

You could then suggest that each partnership decide on something that could enrich their process—a mentor text, a chart—and that they put that resource out beside them (have small copies of the charts on hand), and remind them of ways resources can help the work they are just about to do.

SHARE

Because this session is the last in the bend, your share can serve as a celebration of "look at all I have learned from George and all these other authors!" The best model for your share will depend on how you have grouped your writers for this session. You could have partnerships tell each other about the mentor author or text they are learning from and give examples of features they have tried in their own writing. You could, instead, have writers share what they learned with the whole class, and collect what everyone has learned on a bulletin board or class chart. No matter how you choose to celebrate, make sure students pause for a moment to look back on all they have accomplished so far as narrative writers.

Good luck!

Lucy, Rachel, and Abby

Using All We Know to Revise

IN THIS SESSION, you'll teach children that writers fix up and publish pieces that they especially love.

GETTING READY

✔ Your writing folder filled with writing you have done (both in demonstrations and a few personal stories you have written). Decide in advance which one you will choose to revise and publish, one that is good but not yet polished.

✔ Students' writing folders, to be brought with them to the rug

✔ Stickers for the children to put on the story they select to fix up and publish and for them to mark parts they want to add to

✔ Strips of paper (revision strips), tape, scissors, and a stapler for revision

OFTEN, WHEN TEACHING upper-grade students or teachers, my colleagues and I say, "Think about one time in your life when writing really worked for you." Almost without fail, every single person will respond by telling the story of a time when he or she was published. "I still remember when the teacher read my story aloud," someone will say, and then add wistfully, "I was an author back then."

Nothing does more than publication to make us feel like we are really truly authors. Therefore, it is crucial to end each unit of study with an author celebration. These needn't be lavish affairs, although even a little pomp and circumstance goes a long way.

Teach children that writers select their best work for publication, and they revisit their work by thinking, "How can I fix this up so it's my very best?"

"Children will be gearing up to share their writing as professional writers do—for an audience."

By now, of course, your students will be pros at revising and sharing their stories, so you will want to convey to them that *this* go at revision, *this* preparation for publication is different. This time, children will be gearing up to share their writing as professional writers do—for an audience—and you'll want them to feel the significance of this event.

COMMON CORE STATE STANDARDS: W.1.3, W.1.5; RFS.1.1, RFS.1.4; SL.1.1, SL.1.2, SL.1.3, SL.1.4, SL.1.5; L.1.1, L.1.2

Using All We Know to Revise

CONNECTION

Use a comparison, such as writers to bakers, to teach students that writers need to make sure their work is just right to share it with the world.

"Writers, have you ever baked cookies at home? Maybe it's a birthday party, and you're going to share the cookies with all your friends. That's when you want to make sure the cookies are just right. You want them to be perfectly heart-shaped and the icing to be smooth and the sprinkles on top to be spread out all over the cookie, not just in a clump. Well, guess what? It is the same thing with writing. Sometimes when we write, we share it without worrying whether it just right. (You guys have been doing that with your partner and in this class all year.) But when writers get ready to publish their books, like George McClements and all the other famous authors we know, they use all they know to make sure that their writing is just right."

❧ **Name the teaching point.**

"Today I want to teach you that writers get ready to publish a story by first choosing one that they want to share with the world. Then they revise it using all they know."

TEACHING AND ACTIVE ENGAGEMENT

Demonstrate how you choose a piece of writing to revise by finding one you love.

"Writers, hold up your folders. Oh my goodness, they are bursting with stories from your lives. I hope you feel enormously proud of yourselves! I've got my folder with me too. And now the day has come to pick one story that I want to fix up and make extra special to publish and share. But how do I pick? Hmm, you know what? I don't remember all the stories I wrote, so I'm going to reread them, and as I do, I'll think, 'Of all these stories, which one is really, really important to me?'"

I picked up a booklet and glanced at it quickly. "This story is about when I fell while running in the park. This isn't my favorite, so I am not going to pick it." I put it to the side and picked up another booklet. "Oh! This is the story about going to the aquarium. I like this one a lot, but I'm not sure it's the best example of all that I've learned to do as a writer.

We try to point out to children that revision is a part of life. They revise all the time and in many ways, from refrosting a cookie to rebuilding a block city to rearmoring an action figure. Revision is already part of childhood life, and if we point that out, then writing revision can hopefully blend in to the rest of their revision habits.

I think I'll add it to the 'no' pile. " I picked up a third booklet, leafed through its pages and smiled. "Ah. Now *this* story about all of us dancing on the bubble wrap is one I truly love. It brings back such a good memory, *and* it's got lots of craft moves in it that I'm excited to share with everyone. Yup, this is the one."

Give students an opportunity to choose a piece to publish, reminding them that writers choose the piece that is really important to them.

"Your turn, writers! Open up your folders and spread out a bit so you can make a 'no' pile. Remember, as you quickly read through your pieces, you'll be thinking, 'Of all these stories, which one is really, really important to me?' Be on the lookout for pieces that show off the writer you've become. When you find that one you absolutely love and want to share with the world, close your folder and put it on top. Put a star sticker on it so we know that this is the one you will be publishing."

I gave students a few minutes to do this work.

Show students how you reread a piece, checking that it both makes sense and incorporates craft.

"We have learned so much about how to make our stories special." I pointed to the two anchor charts, "Ways to Bring Stories to Life" and to the craft chart, and said, "We've learned how to write in itsy-bitsy spider steps, how to unfreeze our people, how to tell what they are thinking and feeling, how to write with exact details and pop-out words, and so much more! Look—it's all up here on these two charts. Let me show you how I use these today to fix up my writing."

Ways to Bring Stories to Life

- "Unfreeze" people—make them move, make them talk
- Tell small steps
- Bring out the inside—make people feel, make people think

Learning Craft Moves from a Mentor Author

What did George McClements do?	Why did he do this?
Wrote ELLIPSES in the middle of a sentence	To build up excitement
Wrote EXACT ACTIONS that people do	To make a movie in the reader's mind
Wrote some words that POP OUT	To tell the reader to read with a strong voice

The charts in your room represent the teaching and learning that has been happening across the unit. Your writers have grown (like your charts have grown) and they've developed a repertoire of strategies for the bigger skills of writing, including ways to elaborate. That is why it is important, especially during this time of final revision, to bring them back to these tools as a reminder of all that they know and should use as they move forward with their writing work.

"First, I'll reread my story."

>Page 1: One afternoon I told the class, "I have a SURPRISE for you. Let's meet on the rug." I went over to the rug and sat in my chair, rubbing my hands together as I waited for the kids to come and sit.
>They all SPED over as fast as they could.

>Page 2: I smiled as the kids sat down on the rug. I covered my mouth with my hand so that I would not tell the surprise too soon.

>Page 3: I unraveled a GIANT piece of bubble wrap. I leaned over and whispered to the class, "We're going to have a dance party."

>Page 4: Pop, Pop, Pop! We all jumped and danced around on the bubbles.

"Let me think. Does it make sense? Hmm, the pictures do match the words. Here I am, on page 1, waiting to tell you my secret. And then on page 2, I'm trying not to say the surprise too soon, but I don't see any of you. I think I'll need to add you watching me. And on page 3, I'm unwrapping the bubble wrap. And on page 4, here we are having a dance party! So now let me see if I left out any words (I quickly reread the story out loud). Sounds good to me. Sounds like a story, too. So yes, it does make sense! I'll just add on to my picture on page 2.

"Now let me think. Is this story as special as it can be? Or do I need to add something to it? I have a feeling that even though there are some things here that make my story lively, like the 'Pop, Pop, Pop,' there is more I could add. Let me look at the chart of ways to bring our stories to life to help me."

I read the chart, thinking aloud what I could try. "Writers, do you see what I'm seeing? I wrote this great little story about this really fun thing we did, but I really didn't write at all about how I was *feeling*. In this part," I pointed to middle of page 1, "I was really excited to tell everyone I had a surprise. I want to show that. So how about this: 'I was so excited that my stomach was making somersaults.'

"I want to add this sentence in between these two lines." I pointed to where I had in mind. "So here's what I can do. I'll write the new sentences on a fresh piece of paper," and I did so. "Then, I can just cut the paper and glue (or staple) in the strip so it goes in the right part of my story." I did this. "Now listen to how my story goes!"

>Page 1: One afternoon I told the class, "I have a SURPRISE for you. Let's meet on the rug." I went over to the rug and sat in my chair, rubbing my hands together as I waited for the kids to come and sit.
>I WAS SO EXCITED THAT MY STOMACH WAS MAKING SOMERSAULTS.
>They all SPED over as fast as they could.

Page 2: I smiled as the kids sat down on the rug. I covered my mouth with my hand so that I would not tell the surprise too soon.

Page 3: I unraveled a GIANT piece of bubble wrap on the rug. I leaned over and whispered to the class, "We're going to have a dance party."

Page 4: Pop, Pop, Pop! We all jumped and danced around on the bubbles.

"See what a difference that revision made to my story?"

Set children up to reread the stories they selected and to look for places to revise.

"Writers, your turn. Put on your revision hats." I pretended to put my own hat on. "Reread the piece you selected, and this time, think, 'Does it make sense?' 'What do I need to fix or add?' Then look at our charts to remind yourselves of ways to revise to make your story come to life and craft moves you can try out. When you find a spot you are going to revise, put a sticker on it so you can remember. Turn to your partner and tell him or her what words you are going to add."

LINK

Send students off to continue revising their stories, reminding them of all the classroom charts and scaffolds they can use for support.

"Keep those revision hats on, writers, because now you are going to continue this work of revising your stories back at your tables. Remember to reread each page and then use the charts to help you add to your story so that it makes a movie in your readers' minds. If you haven't yet made people talk in your story, or move, do that! Or you may want to tell what people are thinking or feeling. That's so important in a story! And you may want to try out one of the craft moves that George McClements used in *Night of the Veggie Monster*. You have lots of choices. Off you go!"

Supporting Writers with Different Types of Revision

YOUR MINILESSON will have set children up to reread, revise, and fix up their writing. In conferences, watch how your children try to reread a piece they wrote earlier. You'll probably want to coach into this rereading just as you normally coach into children's reading. "Point under the words," you'll say. "Did it match? Try again." If you can get children to reread their writing with one-to-one matching, this will reveal places where they have left out words or need to clarify meaning.

While many of your writers will revise by adding words and sentences, sometimes even an entire page, there may be writers who need support in deleting parts of their books. This may be because they repeat words or even entire sentences. This happens when writers spend a great deal of time constructing words and lose track of what they've written or when they pick up a piece from the previous writing workshop session and forget to reread before they continue writing. Encourage writers to cross out rather than erase. They can always get a strip of paper (a revision strip) to add more, and erasing takes too much time. Also, you want to celebrate the revision writers are doing, and if something is erased then it is difficult to see the growth in their writing process.

Many of your writers will be adding to their stories to provide more detail for the reader. Use what you know about the writer to help decide how to lift the level of their work. Consulting the narrative writing progression might help you group writers and focus your coaching. Some writers need support using the picture to help them add to their words. Other writers include action and dialogue but will need support telling the internal story. You might also have some writers who are moving closer to Grade 2 on the learning progression and can probably be supported in doing higher-level work around revealing the heart of the story—showing, not telling, and including character thoughts.

MID-WORKSHOP TEACHING   **Stretching Out the Most Important Parts of Stories with Details**

"Writers, can I have your eyes and attention? Writers often revise by finding the most important part of their story and adding details to that part. You are going to do this with the help of your partner. Let's take a break from writing now for a few minutes so that you can reread your stories. When you find *the most important part* of your story, put a star right next to it." The children did this quietly as I walked around and assisted.

"Now, will you share your stories with your partners? Listening partners, you have a special job. When your partner gets to the most important part of his or her story, really try to imagine it so you can ask questions. As your partner reads, think, 'What do I want to know more about? What is missing from this story?' Remember, you can ask your partner who, where, when, and how."

As the partnerships took turns reading their stories and asking each other questions, I conferred to guide their questioning.

"Some writers realize they need revision strips so they have enough space to add words. Some writers have so much more to say that they even took a page out and then write a new page! As you work, think about the questions your partner asked and answer them in your story."

As Students Continue Working . . .

"Writers, once you are done revising this piece, try revising another piece."

Sharing Revision Work

Ask writers to share their stories with their partners, showing their partners where they've revised their writing to make it even better.

"Writers, you need to give yourselves a huge pat on the back because you each fixed your stories up so that they are even better, just like famous authors do. Right now, to see how your story sounds, will you read it to your partner and show him or her where in it you revised? You might want to use our narrative writing checklist to point to specific revisions you made. Remember to read your story with your very best storytelling voice."

"I made the people talk in this part," George exclaimed to his partner. "I added the words I said and then told what my dad said." (See Figure 18–1.)

Ask writers to consider one more revision they can make.

"Remember, partners help each other make their writing better and better. Now that you listened to what your partner did to revise his or her story, think of what else *you* think your partner can add or change to make the story even better for the reader. Did you hear feelings, people talking, the exact actions of what people were doing with their bodies? Use our class charts and our narrative writing checklist if you need help and make a plan for tomorrow."

Once me and my dad took a walk to the park.

And then we sat on the soccer field to relax.

Then we saw a falcon soaring in the air. "Look," I said. "It's beautiful." My dad said, "I agree."

FIG. 18–1   George's story about going to the park with his dad shows revision in strips.

Editing with a Checklist

Y OUR CHILDREN HAVE REVISED their stories to create images in their readers' minds. Their stories are full of what they have learned—pictures, details, dialogue, and action words. Today they will look at their stories again through an editor's lens. The goal is for your writers to understand that editing makes their stories easier to read; editing also means fixing up spelling and punctuation.

Your children will probably have learned how to use an editing checklist in kindergarten. This session will revisit those points and add new expectations for first grade. One of the new expectations for first-graders that this unit addresses is using end marks. (Using capital letters for dates and names of people is another new expectation in first grade, but this will be addressed later in the year in the realistic fiction unit.) By bringing together what they've been learning in writing workshop, word study, and reading, you will show them how to check their pages one at a time and lift the level of their spelling work. They will use one small checklist for each page of their book as a way to guide their editing process. After each page, they will tape the checklist to the back to signal that they completed the editing of that page.

Today, as a mid-workshop teaching point, you will introduce a new spelling strategy—writing tricky words with different spellings and asking, "Which one looks right?" Although your writers may not be studying long vowel patterns now, they do know some of these patterns from sight words and from their own reading. Children will learn to tell when something looks right. For example, most of your writers probably have an image of the word *elevator* somewhere in their mental filing cabinet, but they might not be able to access it readily yet. If they make several attempts to write the word (*elivater, elevater, elevator*), they may be able to figure out some word patterns that bring them closer to conventional spelling.

IN THIS SESSION, you'll teach children that writers reread their writing using an editing checklist, to remind themselves of all the ways they know how to make their writing easy to read for their readers.

GETTING READY

✔ An anonymous student's story that needs to be edited, ideally a Small Moment story written by a first-grade writer. You will use this piece to model editing.

✔ Editing Checklist, prewritten (see Teaching)

✔ Students' selected pieces to publish and pencils, to be brought to the meeting area (see Active Engagement)

✔ Small copies of the Editing Checklist, enough for each child to have one per page of their book (see Active Engagement)

✔ Tape for attaching editing checklists to the back of each student's page

COMMON CORE STATE STANDARDS: W.1.3, W.1.5; RFS.1.2; SL.1.1; L.1.1, L.1.2.b,d,e

Editing with a Checklist

CONNECTION

Use a metaphor to remind children that their writing should be easy to read.

"Writers, have you ever been tricked by a cookie? You see it lying there on the plate, brown and scrumptious and ready to eat, and then when you take a bite," I crunched into an invisible cookie, "Ow! That cookie is as hard as a rock! Nobody wants cookies that are too hard to eat. Cookies need to be baked just right so that they are easy to eat. It is the same thing with writing. Your writing should be easy to read. You work so hard, pouring your hearts into your stories, you don't want readers to say, 'This is too hard to read.' Using neat handwriting is important when you write your story, but that is not really what makes a story easy to read. What makes a story easy to read is careful spelling, spaces between the words, and ending punctuation."

❖ **Name the teaching point.**

"Today I am going to teach you that when writers are ready to publish, they make sure their writing is easy to read. One way they do this is to use an editing checklist that reminds them of all that they know about helping readers read their stories."

TEACHING

Explain that you have a first-grade friend who needs help editing a piece she is getting ready to publish. Demonstrate editing the mystery piece using an editing checklist.

"When you go back and fix your writing to make it easy to read, it is called *editing*. I know a very special first-grader in another school, Anna. She is getting ready to publish her story, but she needs help editing. She can't be here today, but she said she would be so, so happy if we could do this part for her. I have made a special Editing Checklist chart to help us. You will be using this checklist for your own stories too." I showed the checklist written up on big chart paper. (See Figure 19–1.) A template of the Editing Checklist is available on the CD-ROM.

"Look here at all of the things you know so far about writing so that your readers can read your stories easily. Let's use this checklist to help us edit Anna's story. Let me read you her story quickly first."

◆ COACHING

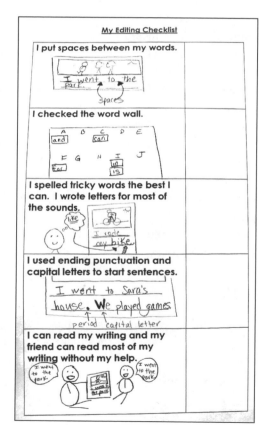

FIG. 19–1   Kid-friendly version of editing checklist

Page 1: One day I playde with the bubls outsid it wuz so fun

Page 2: Then my sister. came outsid she sed can I play with you? I sed yes. she strted bloing bubls We we running all around. There were bubls all over the bakyrd.

Page 3: Then my brothr came outsid to blow bubls too. He strted POPING them. I said no dont pop the bubls but then my sistr POPT them too and I popt them. We were so happy becus it was so fun but then. we had to go in.

"Watch me as I begin to edit Anna's story. I will read one page and then stop and go down the checklist, making sure that I do each number on the checklist."

I reread the first page:

> One day I playde with the bubls outsid it wuz fun.

I said to the class, "I am going to pretend this is my writing as I work on the checklist. The first number on the checklist says, 'I put spaces between my words.' I can see that there are spaces between all the words on this page. I don't have to make any changes. When I finish something on the editing checklist, I check it off!

My Editing Checklist

☐ I put spaces between my words.

☐ I checked the word wall.

☐ I spelled tricky words the best I can. I wrote letters for most of the sounds.

☐ I used ending punctuation and capital letters to start sentences.

"Next it says, 'I checked the word wall.' I know that some of the words Anna used are on the word wall, so I am going to make sure those words in the booklet match the ones on the word wall." I read the line again. "I know *one* is on the word wall, so let me make sure she spelled it correctly in the booklet." I looked at the spelling of *one* on the world wall. "*O-n-e*, yup, she spelled it correctly. I also see *wuz* in her booklet, but on the word wall it is *w-a-s*, so I will have to change that in the story." I took down the word *was* from the word wall and then found the word in the story. I crossed out the original spelling and wrote the new spelling above it. "Anna hasn't used any other words from the word wall, so I am done with this one and can check this off the list." I checked off item 2.

"Next it says, 'I spelled tricky words the best I can. I wrote letters for most of the sounds.' Working hard to spell tricky words means trying to hear as many of the sounds as you can and trying different spellings. It does look like Anna worked hard to spell the tricky words like *bubbles* and *outside*, so I am going to put a check.

"The fourth one says, 'I used ending punctuation and capital letters to start sentences.' This is important. I have to be sure I show readers where my sentences stop and my new ideas begin." I reread the first page aloud. "'One day I played with the bubbles outside.'" I stopped.

Notice how I demonstrate checking all the words I've written, even when I already did the work earlier (i.e., spelling tricky words the best I can). It is important to show children that rereading and really checking before moving on is a way to edit carefully and thoroughly.

"Wait, that is the end of a complete thought. I am going to put a period after *outside* and start the next word with a capital letter." I wrote a capital *I* in the word *It* and read on. "'It was so fun' I should put a period after *It was so fun* because that is the end of the thought." I put a period after *fun* and checked item 4 off the list.

"The last part of the checklist says, 'I can read my writing.' Let's see, does this whole page read smoothly?" I mouthed the words on the page and nodded. "I can read everything smoothly, so let me see if my friend can read my writing," I said as I pointed to the checklist. I called Brendan up to read it. He pointed under each word as he read it, and then turned around and said, "Yup, I can read it," when he was done. "Great," I said. "I'll check the last box.

"I have checked off every box for page 1, so now I can turn the page over and tape on my checklist."

Debrief, reminding children of the steps to use for the editing checklist.

"Did you see how I used the editing checklist to make this story easier to read? I read just one page, stopped, then checked that page using my list. Each time I finished part of the list I checked it off. When I was done with the list for page 1, I moved on to page 2."

ACTIVE ENGAGEMENT

Recruit children to begin editing the first page of their own selected stories, using the checklist.

"Writers, if you still have your revision hats on, take them off and put on your editing hats! You are now going to begin editing the first page of the story you are publishing. Put your booklet and pencil in front of you as I hand out a small editing checklist for the first page of your story. Reread that page and then go down the checklist, starting at number 1."

As children turned to this task, I knelt down and conferred briefly with writers, directing them to the word wall, helping them problem solve tricky words, and reminding them to make spaces between words. Before their scribbling pencils stalled, I reconvened the class.

LINK

Tell children to use the editing checklist to get their stories ready to publish. Remind them to use spelling and ending punctuation strategies also to edit future pieces.

"Remember that when professional writers get ready to share their stories with the world, they work hard to make them just right. They make sure that writing is easy for readers to read. From now on, when you have chosen that special piece to publish, edit it using a checklist, even if the checklist is only in your mind. This will remind you of all you know about making your writing easy for readers to read, like end marks, careful spelling, and spaces between words.

"When your table is called, go to your seat and continue editing the first page of your story. Check off each item on the checklist when you finish it. Then get another small checklist and continue with the second page."

Supporting Students in Their Editing Work
Spelling and Conventions

WHILE YOUR TEACHING TODAY supported your writers in editing their work, you know that there are groups of students who will need support with specific aspects of using language conventions. Today is a great opportunity to support students on this in small groups.

At the same time, for most of your students the priority will probably be spelling. Some of these writers may have been having difficulty reading back their own writing. This may be because only part of the word is represented and the child needs support hearing and recording all the sounds in a word, or it may be a matter of hearing and

---

MID-WORKSHOP TEACHING   Trying Tricky Words a Few Times before Deciding which Way to Write Them

"Writers, I see you rereading each page carefully, checking to make sure you have done all the things we know writers do to make their stories easy to read. I know some of you have gotten to words you know don't look right and are trying to figure out how to write the word the way you know it is written in books you read. I'm going to show you a trick writers use to figure out how a word is spelled. Writers can look at the word and then take out a piece of paper or a white board and try to write the word different ways until it looks right. Myles is working on the word *deep*, trying to figure out which letter or letters go in the middle. Let's try it. He wrote 'dep' on his paper. Let's write it on our white boards. Now let's look at it. Does it look right?"

"Nooo," cried many of the children.

"Okay, so it doesn't look right in the middle. Let's say it, listen to the part in the middle, and think about what other letter or letters make that sound." We said the word again, hearing the long *e* sound. "Writers, we know that sometimes vowels make different sounds, instead of the short sound, they make the long sound—they say their name."

"Put an *e* at the end," announced one writer.

I wrote "depe" under "dep." "Write it on your boards. Don't change the first word because we want to see which way is the way it looks in a book. Does that look right?" Some children shook their heads. Others weren't very sure and continued

to look at it, trying to think about whether they had seen that exact word before. "What's another way to spell *e*?"

"Two *e*'s like *bee*," said one child, pointing to the word wall.

"Let's try that. Everyone write two *e*'s in the middle. Now let's look back at each one. Right away, we all knew the first one didn't look right. We can cross that off. Now, let's look at our second try. Some of you weren't sure about that. Think about if you've seen the word before." More heads shook. "Let's look at our last try to see which one looks the most familiar to us. Does this look right?" I pointed to the last spelling—*deep*.

"Yes," chorused many children.

"So let's cross out the middle try. Now we know which one should go in Myles's book. Myles, can you cross out *d-e-p* in your story and write *d-e-e-p*? Writers make sure they cross out the whole word when they fix the spelling. That helps us and the reader see the word clearly, with all the letters right next to each other."

"Okay, writers, this is something you can be doing now as you check each page and work on spelling tricky words the best you can. Do what Myles did right now and look for a word on the page you are on that doesn't look quite right. Point to it. Now say it and look at it, thinking about which part doesn't look quite right. Say it and try to spell it a different way on your white board. Write it a few ways and then circle the one that looks right and fix it in your story."

---

recording sounds in sequence. Continue to coach these writers to say words slowly again and again until they can hear individual sounds. For these writers, bringing in tools from word study is important, including an alphabet chart or spelling feature charts, sound boxes, or a white board. It might be helpful for these writers to problem solve some of their words on a white board, where they have more space to slide their finger as they say and record the sounds. Another support strategy for these writers might be helping them find places in their stories where they have written challenging words so that they can spell the same word quickly on another page. All they have to do is look back to see how they spelled it.

Other writers who need work on spelling may be writers who problem solve most of their words, which often means their high-frequency words are spelled phonetically rather than conventionally. These writers need support monitoring as they reread in the same way that you support them when reading their books from their book bag. Have children practice reading their writing, stopping at the snap words, and asking themselves, "Does that look right?" If they don't know for sure, they need to check the word wall. Just like you do when they are reading, make your prompts more specific as needed. If the child says it looks right and you know they know the word, prompt them to look at a certain part of the word. For example, if a child spelled *look* as *luk*, prompt him to look at the middle of the word. Does that look right in the middle? If needed, provide a few steps for support: look at the word wall, snap a picture in your mind of the word, and now look back at the word in your book.

While the share at the end of today's lesson provides writers with an opportunity to work with partners, you may pull a few partnerships together sooner who you think

will benefit from this work. These are writers who race through the editing process and need another writer's eyes on the text as they reread to help them monitor for the different skills on the checklist. You can coach them to reread each other's work slowly, pointing together under each word, stopping anytime something isn't quite right. If there is a specific skill that you know a writer needs support with, then guide the partnership toward checking for it. Checking word wall words as well as using end punctuation are two skills that partnerships often work on successfully.

You may still have some writers working toward writing with spaces between words or appropriate use of uppercase and lowercase letters. When coaching these writers, it may be beneficial to have them rewrite a couple sentences as they edit. You might have them identify a part that is missing spaces or that has a mix of uppercase and lowercase letters and then use a page from your own writing to show how you write it again, thinking about making it easy for the reader to read. This might mean taping a strip of paper over this part once they finish rewriting the sentence or sentences. Remember that it is not important that they rewrite the entire piece, because this would probably take too long. The important thing is they get practice doing the work you want them to do with more proficiency as they begin writing in the next unit of study. During any small-group session or individual conference today, know that you will probably be emphasizing one aspect of the editing work more than others depending on the priorities you have set for particular writers. The products may not be perfect, but remember that you are providing important practice opportunities that will strengthen the writers' processes as they write new pieces. This is only the first unit, and with each unit you will expect writers to take on more of the language conventions work. Right now celebrate their approximations in all aspects of the writing work.

Partners Can Be Editors

Ask children to help their partners by rereading their stories and saying what can be fixed up.

"Writers, you did a wonderful job editing your stories by using the checklist. But writers don't write alone. Published books, like *Night of the Veggie Monster* or *Leo the Late Bloomer* and all the other books you see in the library are each written by an author, and then the author edits it, and *then* a different editor edits it again. Partners, you are going to be each other's editors. Read each other's stories and go down the checklist to see if there is anything else to change. If you see something else that your partner can fix up in his or her story, tell your partner so that he or she can make those changes."

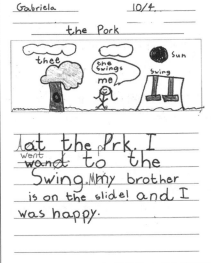

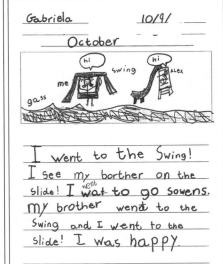

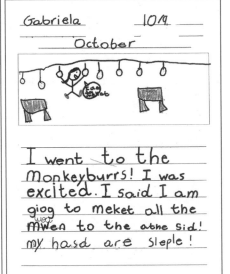

FIG. 19–2   Gabriela edits her writing after partner feedback.

Making Books Ready
for the Library

IN THIS SESSION, you'll teach children that writers get their books ready to publish by including a title, detailed pictures, and a cover.

GETTING READY

✔ Children's selected pieces to publish and a pencil, to be brought to the meeting area

✔ A blank page for each child to make a cover page. The page might be oak tag for durability if you prefer.

✔ Colored pencils, markers, or crayons on each writing table

✔ A piece of paper with a few empty lines in the middle of the page for the back-of-book blurb ✖

✔ An empty basket labeled "Our Small Moments" placed in the classroom library

COMMON CORE STATE STANDARDS: W.1.3, W.1.5, W.1.6; RFS.1.1, RFS.1.4.b; SL.1.1, SL1.5; L.1.1, L.1.2

YOU AND YOUR WRITERS have come a long way since the beginning of the school year. You've undoubtedly seen great progress in your students. They are writing longer down the page, for longer periods of time, and with richer detail and description. There are so many things to celebrate at the end of this first unit, but before that, you'll want to take the writing time today to teach students how professional writers prepare for publication. You'll tell students, "Just as professional writers prepare their stories for the world, so do we." Children, of course, will be enthralled with the idea of becoming published writers and will tackle the final work of the unit with great gusto and enthusiasm.

The focus of this session will be to prepare children's books for the classroom library. What greater honor to a child than to think that his own book will be a part of the classroom library? You will want to convey the message that when a book is ready to be published, a lot goes into it even after the writing is done. Authors come up with a title and cover page, add detail and color to their illustrations, and more. They do all of these things not only to make their books beautiful, but also to let their readers know what their book is all about.

Today's session is a little different from the architecture of most other minilessons. Today children will do a guided inquiry minilesson. They will notice and name what the mentor author does that they have not yet done in their books. While you will prompt them a little, students should be doing most of the questioning and naming themselves, figuring out not just *what* published authors do, but *how*. This minilesson is also different in that students will do two short bursts of independent work. First, they will come up with a title that hints at what their book is about and entices the reader and will design and illustrate a cover page. Then, they will add colors and details to their illustrations to bring out the details of their story. They will plan this work quickly on the rug and then go off to do it before reconvening at the rug, and repeating the pattern a second time. This workshop might take a little longer than usual, but children should be able to keep the momentum as the focus keeps shifting. By the end of writing time, they will have designed beautiful covers and illustrations and will be ready to show their books to the world.

Making Books Ready for the Library

CONNECTION

Tell children that their books are almost ready to publish, but still need finishing touches.

"Writers, tomorrow we will have a writing celebration where we'll share our books with each other. How exciting! And after that, we will put our books in the basket in the library for everyone to read!" I pointed to an empty basket labeled "Our Small Moments."

"That is why I took your writing home with me last night. I was looking at your writing, thinking, 'What is there left to do so that these books are ready to go into readers' hands?' I looked at our mentor texts and I looked at your writing and even the class story we are publishing, and I could easily see what you had done to make your books *sound* like published books. Your books are about tiny seed ideas, just like *Night of the Veggie Monster*. Your books have pictures just like our mentor texts. Your books even have action and characters' thoughts and feelings. Then I thought that even though your books *sound* like published books, they don't yet *look* like published books. And so I thought today we could work together to figure out what you need to do to make your books look like our mentor texts."

Name the teaching point.

"Today I want to teach you that writers put a lot of finishing touches on their books so that these are ready to go in the library for others to read. If writers aren't sure what to do, they can look at a mentor text."

TEACHING AND ACTIVE ENGAGEMENT

Set writers up to investigate the cover of the mentor text, guessing how the author created it.

"Writers, let's look at the cover of George McClements's book. What do you see on the cover that might be missing from your books?" Children began calling out, "Pictures!" Jesse called out, "A title!" "Yes, you're absolutely right. George has a title on the cover of his book and a picture, two things that are missing from your books. We'll need to add those. But first, let's think about *how* George decided on this title and this picture."

◆ COACHING

"Why not just tell the children to make covers, make illustrations, make About-the-Author bios?" you may be asking. And this is an excellent question. My answer is this: our goal is not to get this one set of pieces of student writing better or finished. Instead, our goal is to teach our children writing habits to serve and last a lifetime. If we simply request that children do something, what have they learned? If we explain, again, that writers look to other writers to learn how to be masters, then children will have somewhere to turn and lessons to learn for a lifetime.

"Writers, can you help me figure out how George McClements came up with the title and picture on the front cover of his book? Hmm, he titled it *Night of the Veggie Monster*. Any ideas?"

"Well, it's about vegetables," Cooper said. "And about a boy turning into a monster!" Brett called out.

"Take a moment to talk with your partner, and then we'll share with the group." As children talked, I flipped back through the book, showing each page to the children. "Think about what is on each page," I voiced over. Then I listened in, coaching students to think about what the whole book is about.

Debrief. Restate what children figured out the author did that they could try too.

"Writers, I heard so many of you talking about how the boy hates eating vegetables, and then Jazmin said that he even felt like he was turning into a monster! And we thought, wow, that is the most exciting part of the book! That's probably why he called his book *Night of The Veggie Monster* and not *I Ate a Pea*. That's just what writers do. They look back through all the pages in their book and think, 'Which title will help my readers understand what my whole book is about *and* get them wanting to read on?' Then they come up with a title, which is just a few words to describe their story.

"I also heard some of you talking about how the picture on the cover is actually a picture from one page in the book." I held it up, pointing to the illustration of the boy looking closely at the pea on his fork. "You remember that picture from the book, right? Why do you think George chose this picture for the cover? Turn and talk."

As students talked, I listened in. After a few moments, I said, "Writers, I heard many of you say that readers want to know if the boy is going to eat the pea. What a great observation! That's probably why George put this picture on the cover. It gets us excited to find out what will happen with the pea! Some writers, like George, use a picture from the book, and other writers draw a new picture for their cover. Either way, they make sure it gets the reader excited to find out what will happen in the story."

Send students off to try this in their own books, reminding them to use what they've learned from the mentor text, in this case to write a title that tells what their whole story is about and to draw a picture that entices.

"Now, writers, it is your turn to try this with your own books. When you're back at your seats, look back at your pages and think about what title would help your reader understand what your *whole* book is about. Which part is the really important or exciting part? Think of a title. Thumbs up when you have an idea. Now look back at each page and ask, 'Does this fit with my title?' If it does, great! If not, try another title. Or you can try out a couple of titles and then pick which one you like best. Then decide which picture you will draw on the cover. It might be a picture from one *page* of your story, or a new picture. Either way, your picture should give your reader clues about what the story is about. You'll only have a few short moments to do this, because then we're going to come back to the rug and get ready to add even more to our books. Off you go!"

Set students up to investigate the illustrations of the mentor text, naming what the author has done.

After reconvening the class on the rug, I said, "Writers, I need your help. I was looking at the illustrations in my story and then I was looking at the illustrations in the book *Night of the Veggie Monster.*" I held up a page of both that highlighted the contrast of illustrations. "What is missing from my story's illustrations?"

Immediately, hands went flying up to answer.

Katherine said, "Your story only has sketches, but *Night of the Veggie Monster* has colors."

I responded, "Oh, you are so right! *Night of the Veggie Monster* has colors and tiny details in the illustrations to make us, the readers, feel like we are there in the story. What details does the illustrator draw?"

Jesse blurted out, "You see the color of his hair. It's brown with those little lines. And you can see his blue shirt." "I see the stripes on his shirt!" called out Skylah as she pointed to the page. "There are his fingernails!" I pointed to the tiny circles drawn on the fingers. "There is the fork flying out of his mouth," said Jesse.

I responded again, "Exactly, the illustrator filled the illustrations with color and added the little details, thinking about the colors, designs, textures (like the lines to show his wavy hair), and important objects in the scene like the fork.

"Take a minute and look at your first-page sketch. Think about what colors and details you would add to make your illustrations come to life for the people reading it. Turn and tell your partner what you will color and what details you will add to the first page."

LINK

Debrief. Restate what children discovered that the illustrator did that they could try too.

"So, writers make sure illustrations have details that bring them to life! You will want to use what we've noticed in this mentor text, thinking about where you were, objects that were there, and what each person was wearing so you can prepare your illustrations for publication. Okay, go ahead!"

Providing Specific Support with Publication Preparation

TODAY IS A GREAT OPPORTUNITY to support writers with specific aspects of the publication process in ways that connect their writing work to their reading work. Whereas the reading-writing connection work done during the last mini-publication in Bend I focused a great deal on word- and sentence-level reading, today's publication work connects to the comprehension work you've presumably been doing with students during reading time. Determining the main topic of a book and being able to retell are key skills, and creating a title requires students to use these reading skills.

While students were on the carpet during the teaching about the title, you probably noticed some students who were saying an entire sentence for their title (sometimes a sentence that sounds like the beginning of their book) or whose title didn't quite match what the story really was all about. You can bring these writers together to give them some extra support, linking the work first to reading. You might have them bring their book bags to the carpet and take out a book to study the title. Ask them to think about why the author gave it the title he or she did. Remind them that the title tells

---

MID-WORKSHOP TEACHING   **Writing Blurbs to Tell Readers What a Book Is All About**

"Writers, I want to teach you something else that writers do to get their books ready for publication. They write back-of-the-book blurbs to grab the reader's interest and tell what their book is about.

"When you go to the library or the bookstore, you can't possibly read every book you see from cover to cover to know if you are interested in it! Well, writers have a special way of solving that problem. Writers write a blurb. A blurb is a few sentences that talk to the readers to get them interested in reading the book. Often, a blurb begins by asking readers a question that gets them interested in the book. The blurb doesn't give away every little thing that happens in the story. The blurb is usually on the back of the book or on the inside cover. Listen to the blurb for *Night of the Veggie Monster*." I read it aloud.

> When just a single pea touches the lips of this determined vegetable hater, he doesn't cry, whine, or refuse to swallow. He turns into a VEG-GIE MONSTER! Ready to smash the chairs! Ready to tip the table! Ready to . . . GULP . . . down his peas?

> This wry and funny story by George McClements is the perfect antidote to dinnertime drama, and it may even inspire a few veggie monsters out there to give peas a chance.

"Did you see how George just wrote a few sentences so that the reader could decide if this is a book she or he would want to read? He didn't write *everything* about the story, giving it all away. He just hinted at what the story is about.

"Now think about your own story. What would you say in your blurb to get people interested in reading your book? Turn and tell your partner how you will start your blurb.

"I know Diego's story is about making the goal to win the soccer game. He is going to start his blurb with the question 'Have you ever made a soccer goal?' There are blank pages of paper on your tables for you to write your blurb. We'll then staple this page to the back of your book. Remember, good blurbs don't give away the whole story. They just hint at what it is about to get the reader's attention."

what the book is all about, and usually that means it connects to the important part. It can be helpful to practice saying what title wouldn't work for the book to help them distinguish between the big idea and small details. Then have them go back to their books to do the same work, trying out different titles, just a few words, and checking to see which one is a big idea. It can be helpful to have them say the title and then turn the pages and ask, "Does this fit with the title?"

For some of your writers, spending time on the illustrations and creating a title that really does connect to the whole of the book will be the big work of the day. For those who already have these aspects of the work in place, spending time on blurb writing will be beneficial (see Mid-Workshop Teaching). These writers will need support with summarizing—no easy task for first-graders at this point in the year. While you might not yet expect your first-grade readers to summarize beyond a straightforward retelling of the events in the story, it is good to practice this skill with their own writing. Teach them to think about the characters and the big thing that happens (usually the problem, important part, or exciting part) and tell the reader that. Then they can decide if they want to give away the ending or just give a couple clues before telling the reader to read to find out what happens. For your writers who are ready to do more sophisticated work, you might bring them together to study the blurbs of a few different texts to decide on craft techniques they can include in their own blurbs to entice readers.

Rehearsing

Teach children that writers practice reading their stories aloud, focusing on expression. Demonstrate with your selected piece.

After convening students back on the rug, I said, "Writers, when I read aloud to you, I use my best storytelling voice so that it sounds like I am telling a story. When writers are getting ready to publish their stories, they practice reading these aloud so that their voices sound like beautiful storytelling voices, not like droning robot voices." I said the last part in a robotic tone. "One trick is to read with expression, changing your voice to go with what is happening in your story. If you are reading a sad part, your voice should sound sad and quiet. If you are reading an exciting part, your voice should sound upbeat, and you might read that part a bit more quickly. As I read our shared class story, pay close attention to how I change my voice to match what is happening." I read my story aloud, making my voice match the tone of each part of the text.

Page 1: One afternoon I told the class, "I have a SURPRISE for you. *(My voice went up.)*
Let's meet on the rug." I went over to the rug and sat in my chair, rubbing my hands together as I waited for the kids to come and sit. I was so excited that my stomach was making somersaults. They all SPED over as fast as they could. *(I read excitedly.)*

Page 2: I smiled as the kids sat down on the rug. I covered my mouth with my hand so that I would not tell the surprise too soon.

Page 3: I unraveled a GIANT piece of bubble wrap on the rug. I leaned over and whispered to the class, "We're going to have a dance party." *(I emphasized the word giant.)*

Page 4: Pop, Pop, Pop! We all jumped and danced around on the bubbles. *(I read pop loudly.)*

"Did you hear how I read just now in my best storytelling voice? And how my voice changed to match the different parts of my story?"

Tell partnerships to take turns reading their stories aloud, using their best storytelling voices.

"Now it is your turn. Take turns with your partner. Each of you read your story to each other, really trying to read it like you are telling the story, not just robotically reading the words on the page. I can't wait to listen as your stories fill the room! When it's your turn to listen, offer your partner feedback and tell him or her what's working especially well."

A Celebration

ear Teachers,

More than anything, I want children to learn that they, too, are writers and that they can take the true details of their lives and put them on the page in ways that will make people gasp and laugh and listen intently and want to hear more. The day that does the most to teach children that they are writers is the day you celebrate children's published work. Therefore, every unit ends with children publishing their writing and sending it out into the world.

As you plan each unit, you will want to decide what the celebration will be and share that plan with your writers, thus building excitement. Sometimes celebrations might be simple occasions in which writers read their writing to each other and applaud. Sometimes writers celebrate by reading to book buddies, and sometimes the families are invited to join in. Some teachers choose to propose a toast to their writers, with juice cup held high, to the amazing growth the writers have made. Other times, the celebration focuses on getting feedback from invited readers, often with a comment sheet for readers to fill out or a time for compliments to be offered. Celebrations often reflect the purpose of the unit such as creating a small Expert Fair when writers finish information books, so that they can teach others all about their topics of expertise. The celebrations will grow in scale and complexity across the year, so you probably want to keep this first publication simple.

You will also want to make plans for how the writing will be displayed. During some celebrations, as in this one, you will make a ceremony out of hanging or placing the books in the viewing space inside the classroom. Instead of displaying the books after the children have gone for the day, you may want to use this time for students to announce the publications of their books to the community, explaining what these books represent in terms of their growth as writers. A quick announcement of the title and the writing work they are proud of will make all members of the classroom community eager to read the published books.

Many teachers make a bulletin board with students after the celebration, entitled something like "Small Moment Stories" or "Stories from Our Lives." This may be the

COMMON CORE STATE STANDARDS: W.1.3; RFS.1.4.b; SL.1.1; L.1.6

board that was created earlier in the unit during one of the mini-celebrations and can now be transformed into a display of the final published pieces. Often, teachers place a photograph of each student with an "About-the-Author" page near his or her story so that readers can find out more about each writer. These various ways of celebrating and displaying the books help students see themselves as writers, which, in turn, motivates them to learn even more about all the things that writers do. However you decide to invite your students to reflect on and display their work, you will have a lasting artifact to refer to as you start your next unit of study.

Since this unit is the first one of the school year, a simple celebration of sharing books in small circles and adding them to the classroom library would make the children feel like the authors they have become, like many they respect and admire. They will have a chance to see their books sit alongside the books they have been studying throughout the unit and especially during the third bend. It can be a reminder to them throughout the year that their books are being enjoyed by readers and their books are also available for writers to study in order to strengthen their own writing.

BEFORE THE CELEBRATION

You may want to decorate the classroom with a vase of flowers at each table or with special "Congratulations to the Small Moment Writers" signs hanging in the room, or anything else to convey a sense of excitement and importance for the writing celebration. You will also want to assign each child to a small group ahead of time, thinking about writers who may not yet have had an opportunity to support each other or hear each other's stories during the unit. You could have a chart for small groups visible on chart paper, simply listing the children in each group. You will probably also want to have an empty library basket labeled "Our Small Moment Stories" in the library area. You will also need each child's published piece of writing, organized by assigned group and ready to be disbursed to the authors.

THE CELEBRATION

You will want to make sure the day has a special feel from the moment the children walk in the room, by sharing in their excitement. You might want to stand near the door as children enter in the morning, greeting each and every one with a special message. "Writers, welcome to our writing celebration! I know we have been preparing for this special day, making our books ready for the library. Finally, all that hard work is going to be celebrated as you share your special books with each other and place them in the new classroom library basket."

You might begin the celebration in the meeting area by explaining how the celebration will go and reminding students about the long, hard work that they did in the writing workshop. You might say something like, "You learned to catch the Small Moments from your lives and to write about them. You took these Small Moments and stretched them long in your writing. You wrote these moments with so many details that any reader can get a really clear picture of the story. You've made your stories come to life! Congratulations and give yourselves a pat on the back."

166

To set up the small-group readings, announce to the children that it is now time for other authors in the classroom to enjoy and learn from the writing they've done. "We will have time to share in small author circles. You will each get a turn to read your story to the group of authors sitting around you. Remember, you practiced yesterday to use your read-aloud voice, making sure that your listeners could really feel like your story is coming to life. Once you have finished reading, listen to compliments they have to share with you. Pay attention to these and enjoy that feeling of accomplishment as you hear what you've worked so hard to do as a writer during our Small Moment unit. When all of the groups are finished reading, we will return to the rug, and here is the biggest moment of the celebration... you are going to become authors in our classroom library, just like all of the authors of all the other books we love to read. I have created a new basket titled 'Our Small Moment Stories.' We will have a ceremony where you will each get a chance to stand in front of the class, announce the book you have published, and celebrate what you are most proud of as a writer."

Then you will send the children off in their assigned groups to begin reading to each other. You might want to hand out their published pieces as they go off in their groups or you may want to call each writer, one by one, to come up and get his or her story. You will want to remind students before they go off that when they share their writing, they use their best storytelling voices and that when they listen to their classmates' stories, as readers, they use their best eyes and ears as listeners, getting ready to name what they like about how the author has written the story.

As the small groups settle in, you will want to circulate, encouraging the listeners to put their own books aside, giving their complete attention to the author who is reading. You may want to sit with your own eager eyes, awaiting the reading to begin. If readers need reminding to read louder or slower, you may want to gesture or signal a change in how they are reading and then give a thumbs up and smile before moving on to the next circle. If listening authors need support in giving the compliments, a quick whisper of some words to help initiate the response such as, "I like the way . . ." or "I notice that you . . ." can support the group in responding to the reading. Often, writers are so excited to share their own stories that one story is read and then immediately the next author pulls out his story and begins reading. Your coaching of writers to give and listen to compliments shows students the value of reflection in a celebration.

AFTER THE CELEBRATION

After students have finished reading their pieces, you will want to reconvene the whole class so that the ceremony of placing the books in the classroom library can begin. You may decide to invite each child up, one by one, to say the title of their book, and one way that they are proud of themselves for their book. Then they can put their story in the new "Our Small Moment Stories" basket in the class library.

You might compare the celebration to a graduation, saying, "Writers, when you graduate from a school, you get to come up in front of people because you worked so hard and you get a big round of applause. Now I am going to call each of you up to put your Small Moment story in *our* classroom library. As each person comes up, let's give them big applause. When you come up, say the title of your book—announce it with a loud and proud voice! You'll also have a chance to share one thing you are proud of about this piece of writing before you place it in the bin. This way, the other authors in the classroom can see all the new books they will be able to read when we have reading time in the library *and* they'll know which books they can turn to and study when they want ideas for how to use details to make their own stories come to life. Right now, think for a moment what you are most proud of about the book you wrote. You may want to think about the charts we have up as a reminder of what we learned to do as Small Moment writers this unit or our checklist that we used to figure out what else we could do in our stories to revise them and make them even better. Fold your hands on your books and look up at me once you are ready to announce your book."

Once the writers are ready, begin the ceremony. You will want to call the first student up and have her read the title of her book, holding it out for the other authors to admire. Then coach her to say what she worked so hard to do as a writer in this particular book. Gesture to the bin in the library where she will place it as the audience erupts into a cheers and applause, excited for the new book they can read. What a wonderfully empowering way to start off the year—giving the children the confidence and pride of being "real writers."

Good luck and enjoy the many different roads you will take in your students' writing lives this year.
Lucy, Rachel, and Abby

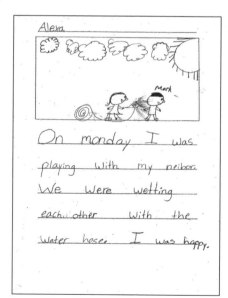
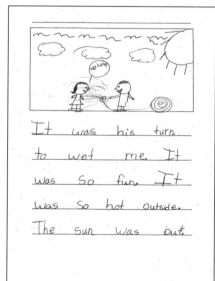
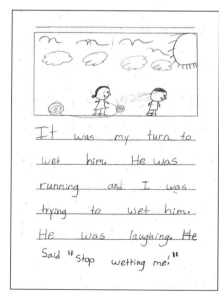

FIG. 21–1   Alexa's story about playing with a water hose in which she shows her strengths in story development—writing both what people say and do and think and feel. She ends by telling the final action and thought.

One day when I was walking home my mom told me my house was full of boxes. We were moving.

I wanted to see how it looks. I was jumping up and down. I was excited.

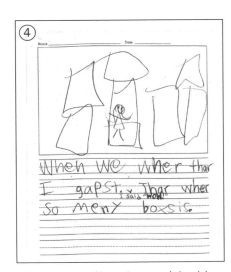

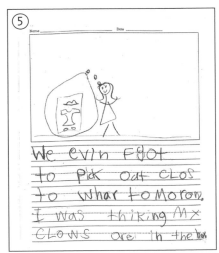

When we were there I gasped. I said "Wow!" There were so many boxes.

We even forgot to pick out clothes to wear tomorrow. I was thinking My clothes are in the box.

And then me and my sister had a snack and then we played hide and seek. It was so fun.

FIG. 21–2 Ella's piece about moving in which she shows her growth in development as she makes her story come to life with actions, feelings, dialogue, and thoughts while also using craft moves such as exact action words like *gasped*. She revises as well as edits for quotation marks and end punctuation in particular.

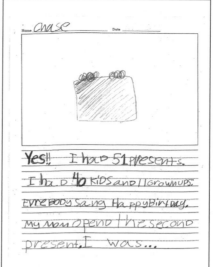

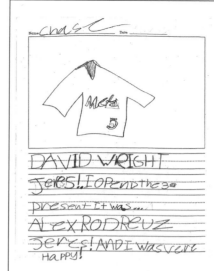

It was my birthday. I found a present. I ripped the wrapping paper. It was a football with a Patriots symbol!! I yelled

Yes!! I had 51 presents. I had 40 kids and 11 grownups. Everybody sang Happy Birthday. My mom opened the second present. It was...

DAVID WRIGHT JERSEY!! I opened the 3rd present. It was... ALEX RODRIGUEZ JERSEY! And I was very happy!

FIG. 21–3 Chase's story about opening presents on his birthday shows how he has become the kind of writer who writes about one time when something important happened to him, makes his stories come to life with feelings and dialogue, and uses craft moves, including pop-out words and exact actions, to create a picture in the reader's mind.